"I have been dedicated ᴛᴏ ___ and I applaud the book *Value Creation Kid*. It highlights the importance of parents being mentors to, not enablers for, their children."

—Sharon Lechter, author of Think and Grow Rich for Women. Co-author of *Exit Rich, Rich Dad Poor Dad, Three Feet From Gold, Outwitting the Devil* and *Success and Something Greater*

"Scott Donnell is passionate about entrepreneurship, and his success at an early age speaks for itself. If you want to prepare your children for a successful and fulfilling life in the 21st Century—and are willing to let them struggle so the lessons they learn are their own, *Value Creation Kid* is all the roadmap you'll need."

—Jeff Sandefer, Entrepreneur & Professor, The Acton School of Business

"This is an inspiring and practical guide to help parents raise money-smart, hard-working kids who are ready to create value for a world that desperately needs it."

—John Lanza, author of *The Art of Allowance*

"This is the book I wish I had when my kids were born. I'm teaching them the principles now and not wasting any more time. It's absolute gold."

—Kary Oberbrunner, CEO, Igniting Souls, *WSJ*, and *USA Today* bestselling author of 12 books

"This book is educational and engaging and is the perfect resource to teach children the basic life skills of managing their money."

—Jim Triggs President and CEO of Money Management International, the largest national non-profit financial counseling agency within the U.S.A.

"*Value Creation Kid* is a goldmine for any parent who wants to raise successful kids!"

—Chad Willardson, Founder & President of Pacific Capital, bestselling author of *Smart, Not Spoiled*

"Scott Donnell and Lee Benson brilliantly focus on developing confident, capable kids prepared to create the greatest value in the world."

—Emily Anne Gullickson M.Ed. J.D. Founder & CEO, A for Arizona

"Scott has cracked the code on helping parents teach their kids money."

—Dr. Benjamin Hardy. Organizational Psychologist and bestselling author

"Scott Donnell is an inspiring force behind a financial education revolution, empowering millions of kids to achieve financial independence and success. Value Creation Kid will help parents better prepare their children for the changes and challenges they face in work and life."

—Jim Kwik, *NYT* bestselling author of *Limitless*

VALUE CREATION KID

THE HEALTHY STRUGGLES
YOUR CHILDREN NEED
TO SUCCEED

VALUE CREATION KID

THE HEALTHY STRUGGLES YOUR CHILDREN NEED TO SUCCEED

SCOTT DONNELL
AND
LEE BENSON

ethos
collective

Published by Ethos Collective™
PO Box 43, Powell, OH 43065
EthosCollective.vip

Library of Congress Control Number: 2023905523
Paperback: 978-1-63680-146-9
Hardcover: 978-1-63680-147-6
Ebook: 978-1-63680-148-3

Available in paperback, hardback, and e-book

DEDICATION

Scott: To my sweet wife, Amy, and our four little value creators. We love getting to watch you grow up.

Lee: And to the millions of kids ready to discover their Value Creation superpowers to change the world. You are our heroes.

"Strive not to be a success, but rather to be of value."

—Albert Einstein

TABLE OF CONTENTS

PART 3
THE REWARD

FOREWORD

Nearly every day, you wake up to a headline about the state of America's children in the wake of the COVID crisis.

A recent report by the Centers for Disease Control and Prevention found 57 percent of teen girls in 2021 reported feeling "persistently sad or hopeless" over the past year, the highest rate seen in the last decade. A third of school children were chronically absent after classrooms re-opened, with many not yet returning to their classrooms. Estimates indicate that millions of students will struggle to ever catch up academically and, on average, face 2–9 percent lower lifetime incomes, depending on the state they live in.

By virtue of the lower-skilled future workforce, states themselves are estimated to face a GDP that is 0.6 to 2.9 percent lower each year for the remainder of the twenty-first century compared to the learning expectations derived from pre-pandemic years. These losses are permanent and will continue to grow unless we invest deeply in the skills our youth need to succeed now.

That's why *Value Creation Kid* is such a critical tool and resource to get into the hands of every parent, teacher, and advocate. There is a purposeful way forward, and the future is bright. Given their shared experiences of life disrupted over the last three formative years, Generation Z and Alpha are already ahead in experiences that help them develop grit, adaptability, and resilience. Scott Donnell and Lee Benson build upon this, providing a critical roadmap to help launch more kids and

1

teens into the world with financial competence, confidence, and a value-creation mindset.

Generation Z is the largest generation ever, accounting for almost 30 percent of the world's population. Globally there are nearly two billion of them, and by 2025, they will make up 27 percent of the workforce. This global generation is highly mobile. They are expected to have 18 jobs across six careers and live in 15 homes in their lifetime. They have integrated technology seamlessly into their lives and are highly visual learners. *Value Creation Kid* outlines actions needed for a strong foundation in adaptability and discovering purpose—both essential traits to create even more value in the world.

This generation feels their K-12 education did not prepare them to enter today's world. They care deeply about the major issues our society is grappling with and want to prioritize family and community first. The authors of this book deeply value the importance of navigating obstacles and challenges to grow in capability, confidence, and value creation—all key traits Gen Z needs to be successful.

Our youngest and future leaders, Generation Alpha, are projected to be the largest generation in the world by 2025. More than 2.7 million Gen Alphas are born each week globally. By 2030, they'll make up 11 percent of the workforce.

Former chief education evangelist to Google, Jaime Casap, regularly challenged audiences to reflect on the problem they want to solve rather than name the job or role they want. Potential roles for this generation include UX manager, drone pilot, blockchain developer, virtual reality engineer, robotics mechanic, AI specialist, urban farmer, and space tourism agent—all roles and industries that did not exist for their millennial and Gen X parents.

Massive changes are already happening in the workforce, and both generations are preparing for jobs, fields, and industries that do not exist yet. Therefore, they must be lifelong learners, holding multiple jobs across multiple careers, constantly upskilling, and retraining to remain relevant to the changes anticipated in working life. That's why the roadmap in *Value Creation Kid* is so essential. It's not optional to be anything other than adaptive and resilient to flourish.

Scott Donnell and Lee Benson brilliantly focus on developing confident, capable kids prepared to create the greatest value in the world. The way these kids will solve problems and meet the needs of the community is aspirational and absolutely achievable. The ripple effect that's possible from grounding our youth in the Value Creation Cycle™ gives me great hope for what the future entails and the problems and broken institutions these young leaders will be able to finally solve.

This book and leadership could not be more timely. I applaud Scott and Lee for putting kids and their futures first.

—Emily Anne Gullickson, M.Ed. J.D.
Founder and CEO of A for Arizona

NOTE TO THE READER

Chances are you've heard the butterfly story.

A man finds a butterfly stuck in a cocoon, trying to break free. He has compassion and doesn't want to see the little creature struggle. Motivated by goodwill and hoping to eliminate pain, the man tears open the cocoon and sets the butterfly free. In the process, the butterfly is limited and forever earth-bound. Nature intended for the butterfly to struggle and strengthen its wings, ensuring a lifetime of flight. By eliminating struggle, the butterfly will never succeed or know its intended destiny.

This is the bedrock of our book.

Motivated by empathy and goodwill, many of us adults remove struggle from the children we love. We tear away the tension and remove their obstacles. Hoping to fast-track them to success, we aim to set them free. But in the process, we clip their wings. Despite our best intentions, unless they struggle, they'll never experience flight or know their intended destinies.

Our children are designed to experience healthy struggles. It's what they need to succeed. By inviting the correct challenges and obstacles, we set them up to win in work and life. Proper tension produces invaluable qualities like grit, discipline, and self-worth. These attributes grow their belief and capabilities, helping them soar into success.

Without healthy struggle, there's no opportunity for capability, confidence, or Value Creation. As a result, there's no chance at true happiness either. Bestselling author Tony Robbins explains why. In an interview with CNBC, Robbins said, "I always tell people if you want to know the secret to happiness, I can give it to you in one word: progress. Progress equals happiness."

Simply put, healthy struggle is an essential part of truly happy kids. We depict this in the Value Creation Cycle™ below:

THE VALUE CREATION CYCLE™

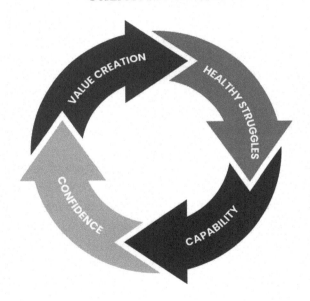

Healthy struggle creates the opportunity for kids to develop new capabilities. Once that new capability is acquired, then confidence is built. This sets the stage for a child to create value from their newly developed capability. Repeating this cycle over time will set children up to create massive value in the world around them. Children need these healthy struggles to succeed while they are young to win as adults.

INTRODUCTION

By reading this book, we know something incredible about you. You care about kids. You might be a parent, a teacher, a grandparent, or a civil servant. Regardless of the title, you value children; because of that truth, we highly value you.

We share your passion, and we believe in a better way and a better world. If you haven't read the Note to the Reader, please do so now. It takes 2 minutes. If you've already read it, we invite you to reread it.

Here's why. In many ways, society is hard-wired to sabotage kids. We insulate and isolate them from struggle, and as a result, we rob them of their chances for success. So instead, we pour on comfort and eliminate challenges. Our intentions are noble, of course. But life is intended to teach children character through challenges and self-esteem through obstacles.

> LIFE IS INTENDED TO TEACH CHILDREN CHARACTER THROUGH CHALLENGES AND SELF-ESTEEM THROUGH OBSTACLES.

Parents say things like:

- I don't want my kids to have to deal with the things I had to deal with as a child.
- I just want my kids to have all the opportunities I never had.
- I want my children to have the stuff that I never had as a kid.

SCOTT DONNELL AND LEE BENSON

Be careful what you wish for because those struggles made you who you are today. Of course, traumatic experiences and unhealthy family patterns should never be passed down from one generation to the next. However, in our effort to protect our children and eliminate all of their struggles, we may be spoiling them and hurting their future.

Let us introduce ourselves—Scott Donnell and Lee Benson. Scott is in his thirties, and his kids are still young. In fact, he and Amy just had a brand-new baby, their fourth child. Lee is in his sixties and has mentored countless teens and young adults throughout his career.

Scott's companies have served millions of kids and families in leadership, fitness, and financial competency. Lee's companies have created jobs for thousands of families, and he serves on the board of several organizations that are creating the future of education.

Despite our differences in age and experience, we've joined together to write this book—*Value Creation Kid*™—and to create a movement—centered on creating financial competency for kids and families so they can generate more success in work and life.

Co-authoring can be tricky. Often, the authors get in the way of their readers.

Who's talking now? Scott or Lee? Announcing the speaker all the time can feel redundant and break up the flow. Also, switching voices back and forth can add to the confusion.

So, to save you sideways energy, and to make you, the reader, a priority, for the most part, we'll write the book as one voice, blending both of our perspectives. If the context demands distinguishing between two voices, then we'll use literary devices like subtitles or section breaks (also called fleurons and better known as the squiggly marks that divide up sections like the one below).

* * *

We're committed to bringing you curated content, proven processes, and relevant truth packaged with practical application. Our vision isn't new words on a page but rather unpacking a new way for our kids to navigate a new world of challenges. This "new way" equips them with the tools to succeed.

Here's what we mean.

We aspire to launch a significantly higher percentage of kids and teens into the world with financial competence, confidence, and a value-creation mindset. When we started our company GravyStack™, we surveyed over one thousand parents and their kids. Almost all the parents said they knew their kids' schools weren't teaching everything they needed to be ready for the real world. The most common responses we heard from parents were:

- I don't have a roadmap to teach my kids about financial competency or how to possess the life skills required to succeed.
- I don't even know where to begin, and I won't know how I did until my kids are twenty-five, thirty, or even forty years old.
- And even if I had a plan, I don't know whether my kids would even listen to me half the time.

This book addresses and answers those concerns.

If you think GravyStack is a weird name, we agree. It is! Here's the quick story of why we chose it. Scott (the Founder) and Travis (a Co-Founder) were on the phone trying to come up with a name for this zany new idea of a bank that plays like a game. Scott loved the word, Gravy. It connects to Gravy Train (money, of course) as well as "all the extras in life." We thought about smashing it together with the word "stack." As people leverage the capability to create more and more value over time, the gravy begins to stack up. "Stacking Gravy" is simply a metaphor for kids to build more value over time. And it's fun to say. Thus the name, GravyStack. When children understand this concept of Value Creation, it's a huge "light-bulb" moment, and the rest is history. Now, our community loves the concept of creating a GravyStack money machine.

GravyStack is the world's most fun bank account for kids. The app plays like a game, and it teaches financial competency and life skills to the next generation. Our mission is simple: create 50 million financially competent kids ready to succeed in the real world. And in the process, we give freedom back to their busy parents.

The GravyStack app includes a hundred fun games and real-life missions. Each one helps kids become financially competent and capable of creating value in the world. Starting from the very first time they use the app, they'll be encouraged to earn, save, and spend wisely, but in a gamified way. Then, as they continue engaging with the app, they'll learn to invest, get challenged to share, and be equipped with how to protect themselves online. All this education is ultimately designed to help them create value at home and in the world around them.

Whether you're a parent, teacher, or coach, there are three ways to use this book effectively:

1. **As a roadmap**. A roadmap is only valuable when there is a clear path toward a goal worth reaching. The goal is to raise confident, capable kids prepared to create value in the world. This is the definition of GravyStack—stacking your gravy or stacking the value you create for yourself and others. GravyStack.com complements the book through practical application. We begin with helping you create a kid's bank account and giving you a system of creating value in the home. Then, your kids

can play over 100 games to help them become financially competent in the world.

2. **As a tool.** A good tool is easy to use and cuts through the noise. Put this book in your toolbelt as you raise and coach your kids to success. The book outlines simple tips and techniques to refer back to. The GravyStack Method™ makes it easy for you and your kids to get on a healthy journey of creating value for your family and the world.

3. **As a mindset.** A mindset is the lens through which you see the world and change your state to excel in that world. The book teaches you and your kids to adopt a mindset of creating value. It's why we were put on this earth. Each child was made for a specific purpose. A shift in one's mindset causes the fastest change and growth in an individual. Your new mindset will shift how you see your world and the opportunities readily available to you and your kids.

We call the ideas and philosophies that make up the banking app, The GravyStack Method. It's a simple, sustainable way to teach your kids to create value in your family and in the world. There are four main building blocks to The GravyStack Method:

THE GRAVYSTACK METHOD™

Value Creation

House Rules

Financial Competency

Healthy Struggle

The GravyStack Method teaches your kids to choose the right perspective when challenges come up. We call these challenges *healthy struggles,* and they should be appreciated, not avoided. Most kids understand that being challenged in academics or athletics is a key component to excelling in school and sports. The same rules apply to life.

MOST KIDS UNDERSTAND THAT BEING CHALLENGED IN ACADEMICS OR ATHLETICS IS A KEY COMPONENT TO EXCELLING IN SCHOOL AND SPORTS.

Experiencing challenges when earning money and creating value is part of the real world. Sheltering kids from this truth doesn't help them. It hurts them. The sooner we can show kids healthy struggles, the sooner they have a chance to understand true success.

Let's be honest. Most adults never learned these important lessons. It takes us years to understand the value of money and how to create value in the world for other people. The only way we learn these truths is through struggle and making mistakes. Most of our parents thought that protecting us from the struggle was the most loving thing to do.

Think back to the butterfly story. Struggle is our friend and teacher. Or perhaps you're old enough to remember the movie *Karate Kid*, the predecessor of the recent series *Cobra Kai*. The young Daniel wanted the fastest path to victory. His mentor, Mr. Miyagi, understood what Daniel needed. He couldn't get there unless he struggled. As a result, he equipped him with a brush and then, later, a sponge. Daniel didn't appreciate the struggle.

In the famous scene, he complains to his sensei, at first, about missing out on going fishing.

Daniel: Hey, how come you didn't tell me you were going fishing?

Mr. Miyagi: You not here when I go.

Daniel: Maybe I would've liked to have gone. You ever think about that?

Mr. Miyagi: You karate training.

Daniel: I'm WHAT?! I'm being your dang slave man is what I'm being! Now we made a deal here.

Mr. Miyagi: So?

Daniel: So? So you're supposed to teach and I'm supposed to learn, remember? For four days, I've been busting my butt and I haven't learned a dang thing!

Mr. Miyagi: Ha, learn plenty!

Daniel: I've learned plenty! I've learned how to sand your decks maybe! How about wash your cars, paint your house, paint your fence. I've learned plenty!

Mr. Miyagi: Oh, Daniel-san, not everything is as seems.

His sensei went on to show him how all the "struggle" of painting a fence and washing a car was an intentional part of his karate training. He "stacked" mental, physical, and heart strength by exerting physical effort. And in his moment of testing, Daniel proved successful.

* * *

The GravyStack Method helps you communicate to children through a value-creation lens rather than a what's-in-it-for-me lens.

Although the book provides practical examples, compelling case studies, and proven strategies, the book works best in conjunction with the GravyStack app. This tool travels with you wherever you go through the convenience of your phone. It can also be accessed through a tablet or computer. Our team is so committed to this concept and to you as caregivers that we want you to give it a test drive. Simply scan the QR Code below or visit GravyStack.com/go, and you'll see what we mean.

PART 1

CHALLENGE

.

CHAPTER 1

START THE VALUE CREATION JOURNEY EARLY

A value-creation mindset will set your kids up for success.

Perhaps you've heard of Failure to Launch (FTL) syndrome. Although it's also the name of a 2006 romantic comedy starring Matthew McConaughey and Sarah Jessica Parker, it's not a laughing matter. More and more young adults are falling prey to FTL syndrome each year. According to *Psychology Today*, the composite profile of an FTL person is as follows:

He is 23 years old and a drop out of college after a semester and is now living at home and totally dependent on his parents financially, as well as on services such as laundry. He isolates himself in his room and often sleeps during the day. Unemployment has a detrimental effect on young adults' psychological well-being. That, coupled with parental financial support, may reduce their psychological resources and their self-efficacy and make the transition to adulthood lengthy and precarious.

Not only does the Value Creation Mindset protect against this issue, but it gives parents the assurance and peace of mind that their kids will have the best chance of success in the world.

Being a parent is hard enough as it is. There's no better way to beat the selfishness out of you than to become a mom or a dad. Parenting is physically exhausting when your kids are young and mentally exhausting when your kids become teenagers.

If you're like most, you never realized how much freedom you had before kids. There was freedom to do what you wanted when you wanted to do it. You could hang out with friends on a whim or spontaneously travel wherever you wanted to go. But once you bring a little human into the world, everything changes. Whether you are prepared for it or not, raising great kids becomes your primary focus. And let's be honest, most of us are in the "not prepared" category at the beginning.

We love our kids and want to see them grow and succeed in the world. Raising kids who enjoy creating more value than they take is one of the most rewarding and difficult challenges we face. Most of us have the same questions that sometimes keep us up at night.

- Am I doing what I am supposed to do to ensure that my kids are prepared to succeed in the world?
- Have I done enough to make them future-proof, so they will be self-reliant and contributors to their family and community, no matter what the circumstances of the future hold?
- Are they learning the right things in school and at home?
- Are they going to be caring, loving contributors to society?
- Do I encourage them to be confident and capable, or am I coddling or spoiling them?

- Am I making life too easy for them that it might delay their ability to create value on their own as adults?
- Did I leave the oven on?

The questions are endless. I am sure I left many out.
But now imagine a home where your kids are:

- focused on creating value in the world instead of worrying about what the world owes them
- givers instead of takers with no fear of the future because they create abundance every day rather than scarcity
- creating value rather than asking you for money
- regularly asking how they can help you
- making great friends and being a valuable friend to others
- never falling prey to the popularity contests, cliques, or social media highlight reels that others try to force on them
- anxious about nothing, and always ready for a good challenge
- always inspiring to be a better version of themselves and loving the journey

This isn't wishful thinking. It's what we hear every day from parents.

We want to help you create a home where other parents want their kids to go because they notice a difference in their kids when they return home. There is little to no conflict in your home, no bribery or coercion to make them do their homework or chores, and no "buying" their affection or compliance. You have full confidence that your kids have learned everything required to thrive when they leave the nest, and you have a sweet and deep relationship with each child. Ultimately, when they look back at their time growing up, they remember it as valuable, loving, and fun.

"How does all of this work," you might wonder. It's because the best value wins!

Creating value gives meaning and purpose to anyone's life. It closes the door to unhealthy thoughts and behaviors that have a negative effect on emotional energy. An education should create value in the world by solving problems or meeting material, emotional, or spiritual needs within individuals, organizations, or the community. The purpose of school is not just to get a good grade, diploma, college degree, or job.

Unfortunately, K-12 education has become synonymous with memorization rather than gaining useful life skills and creating value. *Imagine if your kids based their primary motivation on the value they create in the world rather than what others think of them.* There are so many forms of judgment for kids today in the physical and virtual worlds. This has led to a rise in social and emotional victim status.

> IMAGINE IF YOUR KIDS BASED THEIR PRIMARY MOTIVATION ON THE VALUE THEY CREATE IN THE WORLD RATHER THAN WHAT OTHERS THINK OF THEM.

When we say that your kids' primary motivation is creating value, we're not talking about being in the cool club, the smartest in the class, or the best at sports. Instead, we're talking about creating positive material, emotional, or spiritual value. It's great, for example, to want to excel at sports. However, it can be dangerous for your kids to wrap too much of who they are into being a good football player. What happens if they get injured or are not good enough to make the team? The Value Creation Kid will continue to thrive in this scenario and simply create more value. Circumstances do not sabotage them. Rather, they transcend them.

What could be different in your family if your kids based their primary motivation on the value they create in the world? When we see the world with a value-creation lens, we immediately see how each type of value can be created from almost any situation, whether material, emotional or spiritual. For kids, this is like a lightbulb turning on in their minds. This causes them to develop a stronger sense of purpose, meaning, and identity.

An identity that comes from creating value is a rock-solid identity that cannot be shaken. When you create value for yourself and those around you, you fortify in yourself a strong sense of self-esteem and self-confidence. No number of affirmations or manifestations could ever touch the type of confidence that comes from creating value. As Alex Hormozi says, "You don't become confident by shouting affirmations in the mirror, but by having a stack of undeniable proof that you are who you say you are."

There are three types of value that can be created:

1. Material Value
2. Emotional value
3. Spiritual Value

Incredible outcomes arise when kids learn value-creation language and the three types of value listed. Over time, they'll discover which value-creation activities resonate the most. Each type of value will be explained later on in this section.

Creating real value in the world has to be done in a win-win way, not win-lose. There should always be positive value created. A simple example is your child agreeing to do something for a neighbor in exchange for pay, such as running errands or mowing their lawn. In this case, your child exchanges their best efforts in doing the requested project or task for pay, and your neighbor saves time in order to do higher-value things. This is a win-win exchange of value.

The obvious opposite would be getting paid to do something and not doing it. This is a win-lose exchange where the loser will likely never engage in the exchange again.

Thinking in terms of Value Creation can be a major shift for most people. This is so important because a win-win exchange of value has no limits to how it can grow or how long it can last. This win-win exchange can even outlast us and pass down through future generations.

When you start early with a win-win intention and mindset, the smallest things will always grow into larger exchanges of value. This story from interviewing a parent (Cyndi Laurin) for this book illustrates the point:

> When I was eight years old, our neighbors had a big Irish Setter named Bernie. The owners, Jack and Pat, were about the same age as my grandparents. Pat would have me come over and brush Bernie for her, which I loved to do, and she would pay me with a small glass of Coke* and a cookie. She and I would sit at her little bistro set and talk. I loved the work, and even more, I loved sitting and talking to Pat. I felt so grown up.

> The "payment" of Coke and a cookie was brilliant. I never missed an opportunity to work for Pat! As I got older, she would have me clean off her back patio or do little things in her garden. Those were really special times. The older I got, the more other neighbors hired me (and paid me money) to babysit, take care of their animals or mail when they went on vacation, wash their cars, etc. I was known as the cul-de-sac handyman. They paid me well, and it made me recognize how helpful it was to them.

The earlier you start the value-creation journey for your kids, the better. Ideally, you can start exposing them to value-creation language from the moment they can speak. But any age will do. Again, here are the three main categories of Value Creation:

1. **Material Value:** The positive value created by what you create and produce.
2. **Emotional Value:** The positive value created by how you think and feel and how you make others think and feel.
3. **Spiritual Value:** The positive value created by how you live and love others and your connection to something greater than yourself.

Material Value

A clear way to think about material value is the *accumulation of your best efforts*. This is where you exchange your best efforts for something of material value. Although we often think of this as money, it can be anything of material value. How much you get paid for your best efforts depends on the perceived value of the person paying you. The more value perceived for your efforts, the more you will be paid. A savings account is really just the accumulation of your best efforts.

Many people believe they are worth more than they are being paid to do a job, and this may be true in some cases. But in each case, the person or company paying them will likely only pay what they perceive the exchange of value to be. The same standard applies both ways. No one willingly pays more than what they perceive the value to be for goods or services.

Each time a good or service is paid for, including getting paid for a job as an employee, material value is exchanged. When you ask any employee how they create value for their organization, they usually struggle to answer. At best, they respond with a job description. It is rarely an answer that describes the value the organization gets in return for paying them. Organizations should receive more value than they pay each employee, or they could go out of business.

The value-creation mindset makes everyone more successful by being more intentional about creating value rather than just going through the motions and missing opportunities. It's amazing how much more value employees, leaders, and companies create when they intentionally create it. Imagine the head start your kids will have by starting them on this value-creation journey early. They will be the most sought-after and valued team members in any organization.

ORGANIZATIONS SHOULD RECEIVE MORE VALUE THAN THEY PAY EACH EMPLOYEE, OR THEY COULD GO OUT OF BUSINESS.

Money often brings up both positive and negative emotions. There are many reasons for this, mostly from perceptions regarding how the money is being used and whether or not it is being distributed fairly. Thinking of money as accumulated best efforts takes away all the negative perceptions. Having conversations with your kids about money through the lens of creating value will improve their relationship with money now and throughout their lives.

Emotional Value

A clear way to think about emotional value is how people feel about themselves and what they can accomplish. When our positive emotional energy runs high, we feel like we can do anything. In this state, we have lots of motivation and drive to be and do more. When our positive emotional energy is running low, we don't have a lot of motivation and can get easily discouraged and frustrated.

The mind is a powerful tool. It controls our thoughts and emotions. It can make us thankful and excited about life, or it can make us miserable. It has the ability to destroy value by blaming others, causing anxiety, and making us feel like victims. But it also has the power to view struggle as an opportunity to learn, to grow, and to make us stronger. Simply put, we have the power to choose how our mind sees the world.

Emotional energy has the power to create and destroy. When people interact with you, and they leave in a higher state of positive emotional energy, you have created more positive emotional energy by giving it to others.

The opposite is a reality too. Have you ever felt great and then interacted with someone who made you feel worse? That person destroyed emotional value. The goal is to always increase positive emotional energy in the world, not reduce it.

We all want to be around people with positive emotional energy. It makes us feel good, remain curious, and explore opportunities.

One of the easiest ways to do this is simply to be intentional. Raising positive emotional energy supercharges everything, including material and spiritual value-creation. High states of positive emotional energy inspire greater output. This is where we find better solutions to problems, and we can do 2–5 times as much in the same amount of time, depending on the activity.

When asked, "What is the scarcest commodity?" most of us would say *time* because you can never get it back. Consider something else. What if positive emotional energy is the scarcest commodity? Think about it. Would you rather live a long life where your emotional energy is only at one or two on a scale from one to ten? Or a 20 percent shorter life where your emotional energy is consistently at a nine or a ten? "Healthspan" is not the same as lifespan. Or another way to say it is this–quantity of life doesn't supersede quality of life.

When you increase positive emotional energy, it does two things: first, it energizes everything you personally do to create value in the world, and as a result, you create that value faster. Second, it allows you to infuse more positive emotional energy into everyone you interact with.

Kids can choose from many careers that center around creating positive emotional value. These include singing, writing, acting, speaking, counseling, teaching, and many more. The possibilities for creating positive emotional value are endless, whether in one-on-one interactions, within groups or at scale.

Think about your favorite popular song that elevates your emotional energy when you hear it. Imagine this song doing the same thing for millions of people. If a child becomes a musician, they have the potential to positively impact the emotional energy of millions of people. The same thing applies to uplifting movies if a child becomes an actor. Creating more emotional value is one of the most important activities we can do.

Spiritual Value

A clear way to think about spiritual value is how you live and love others and how you connect to something greater than yourself. When spiritual value is created, people take the focus off themselves and connect with something much bigger. This larger mission provides us with a sense of purpose.

Creating spiritual value requires us to shift from self to service. Most toddlers and young children can act as if they are the center of the solar system. They don't understand there's a bigger world outside of themselves.

There's an explanation for this, and it centers on brain development, specifically within the prefrontal cortex. This is the last part of the brain to develop—it centers on impulse control, emotional regulation, problem-solving, and flexible thinking. One of the best signs of maturity in children and teens is their ability to learn and practice empathy, compassion, and selflessness. Sadly, some people never even reach this stage. We call them narcissists.

As we develop in this area, we begin to ask deep questions.

- Why am I here?
- Who created all this?
- Is there a purpose for my life?
- Where should I invest my time?

By wrestling with these questions, we can find purpose, and when we do, we have the opportunity to create spiritual value. This value is the net positive of how we love and serve others and connect ourselves and others to something greater. The degree of value is personal to everyone, and their ability to lift others up also varies.

People create spiritual value in different ways. For me (Scott), as a Christian, my identity is in Christ. This simply means that God made me, he loves me, and he has a purpose for my life to bring value to others. My worth is not determined by how much good I do, and I can't earn my way to heaven. Jesus did that for us. But now, we have total freedom to create value for others as a reflection of the creative God who made us and is in us.

I think that we were all made to create value. I love how the Apostle Paul puts it: "For we are God's handiwork, created in Christ Jesus to do good works, which God prepared in advance for us to do" (Ephesians 2:10, NIV).

You are valuable because God made you. And when you mess up, there's forgiveness. This gives you the freedom to love, serve, and encourage others without trying to meet some sort of quota. You can now spend your life lifting others up. That is what creates spiritual value.

* * *

One of the greatest signs of creating spiritual value is joy. When we connect to something or someone beyond ourselves, there's an immediate sense of relief and release. Helping others do this creates even more joy—for others and for ourselves.

Joy comes when you realize it's not all about you, it's not always as it seems, and it's not all up to you to fix it. When you realize you have a greater purpose, the weight falls off. Letting go of control and changing our perspective frees us. This is the benefit of creating spiritual value—true joy.

Happiness differs from joy. Happiness is a momentary feeling resulting from your current circumstances. It's fleeting. The moment your circumstances change, your happiness is gone. How many times has your momentary happiness been ruined by a change in your circumstances or surroundings?

- You're enjoying playing in the yard with your kids, but then they start to argue or fight about a toy or who gets the next turn.
- A great business meeting is followed by rush-hour traffic.
- The birthday party you planned so long for and the presents you so lovingly purchased and wrapped turn into a madhouse of crazy kids on a sugar-high fighting over the piñata bat.
- You finally get that year-end bonus, but then you get a call from a relative saying that the cancer is back.
- The perfect date night with your significant other is ruined when one of you brings up the budget, a kid problem, a past relationship, or a job frustration.

Here's a pro tip for the perfect date night: date nights should have no phones, and set ground rules beforehand for it being either a Fun Date with no discussion of issues or calendars or a Fact Date to plan and discuss things together.

Happiness dissipates.

Happiness comes and goes. Culture wants us to pursue happiness now, to seek instant gratification on social media, on Amazon, or with more pills, more sugar, and more dopamine. It's how they keep us hooked, and it's how they make their money.

Joy, however, is different.

Joy is only experienced when you can let go of the current circumstances and see the bigger purpose for your life. Contentment and peace quickly follow. The greatest way to reduce stress and endure struggle is by gaining a higher perspective for your life and connecting to something or someone greater.

THE VALUE CREATION KID USES HEALTHY STRUGGLES TO CREATE VALUE, AND IN DOING SO, THEY FIND JOY.

Whenever I get into a difficult situation or struggle—sick kids, sleepless nights, marriage issues, lawsuits, website crashes, threats from competition, health issues—I'm able to quickly reframe the problem into an opportunity to create value. I give up thinking that I have to do it all right now and that I have to bear all the weight on my shoulders. I keep these words in mind:

> Not only that, but we rejoice in our sufferings, knowing that suffering produces endurance, and endurance produces character, and character produces hope, and hope does not put us to shame, because God's love has been poured into our hearts through the Holy Spirit who has been given to us (Romans 5:3-5, ESV).

The potential to create spiritual value begins when we realize things are not happening *to* us but *for* us. We create spiritual value for others as we encourage them, lift them up, love them, and remind them there is more in store for their life than the current struggles they face.

* * *

When most people hear the idea of creating value, they immediately think of money. However, money is merely the outcome of producing material value. Money is one type of measuring stick for Value Creation, and it should be kept in its proper place. It's a storage place for value that can be useful for buying things that you want or need, but it's not an end in itself. There are also many things more valuable than money, such as relationships, love, and physical and mental health. There are also memories, experiences, or anything you consider "priceless." Some things money can't buy. For everything else, there's GravyStack.

Most people spend time trying to earn more money rather than create more value. We can get caught up living paycheck to paycheck—or worse, suffering in debt. It's easy to fall prey and waste mental energy worrying about paying the bills, keeping a roof over our heads, putting food on the table, buying stuff we want, and hopefully, having a little bit left over before we die.

The temptation is to exchange time and effort for money rather than focusing on creating more and more value in the world.

MOST PEOPLE SPEND TIME TRYING TO EARN MORE MONEY RATHER THAN CREATE MORE VALUE

The good news is we've seen a new reality when people understand and apply The GravyStack Method. With a change in mindset, the next biggest jump in your career could come from focusing on creating maximum value for those around you instead of focusing on how to get a small pay increase next year.

30

Promotions almost always go to the value-creation detective that finds ways to build and grow value on their own without being told.

Looking through this lens of the world, life becomes very simple. These two questions will help guide you:

- Does this decision add value to myself and others?
- Is what I'm doing right now adding the maximum value it could, or could I invest my energy in a more valuable way?

The value-creation mindset is a stacking mindset, meaning it compounds the more you use it. Every situation, conversation, decision, and task becomes a new opportunity to add that much more value to yourself and others, whether it comes in the form of material value, emotional value, or spiritual value.

High-Value Takeaways:

- Healthy struggle is required to create more value in the future.
- Start early: It is never too young to start your kids on their value-creation journey.
- Start with adding value-creation language into your family conversations and use GravyStack.com as a tool to make the process fun for kids and less work for parents.
- Material value: Exchange your best efforts for the accumulated best efforts of others in the form of money.
- Emotional value: Create a net positive emotional energy that supercharges all things.
- Spiritual value: Live, love, and connect to something greater than yourself.

CHAPTER 2

STRUGGLE DOES NOT EQUAL TRAUMA

Making it too easy can make it much worse.

One of parents' biggest fears is that their kids will get traumatized or screwed up somehow from their childhood, and it will be all their fault. Their response is to try and eliminate struggle from their children's lives. Parents avoid conflict wherever possible, remove obstacles, avoid difficult conversations, give in to their kids, coddle them, and run to their aid when they seem frustrated or stuck. Parents don't realize that struggle is unavoidable and often required for growth in the real world. Delaying their struggle now only delays their growth later. The key is to help them struggle well and be an anchor for them in the process.

DELAYING THEIR STRUGGLE NOW ONLY DELAYS THEIR GROWTH LATER.

There's a reason why no great movie or great book ever made didn't have some sort of epic struggle. Struggle is required for growth, and overcoming adversity is what builds true character. That is what makes a movie character so memorable.

We want to be courageous like William Wallace in *Braveheart*, strong like Maximus in *Gladiator*, brave like Anna from *Frozen*, and resilient like characters from *The Pursuit of Happiness*, *The Shawshank Redemption*, *Rocky*, *Batman*, *The Avengers*, *Forrest Gump*, *The Lord of the Rings* series, and *The Lion King*. The list is endless. We gravitate to these examples and aspire to emulate their ability to overcome struggles, rebound, persevere, and come back stronger.

So, how do we help our kids go through healthy struggles without traumatizing them?

I was recently speaking to a friend whose daughter was in college. He was so proud that she called him almost every week. But then I asked him what they talked about, and he started thinking. He said that the last five conversations were as follows:

- She needed him to pay off the credit card because it was maxed.
- She needed him to call the car insurance company because she forgot to pay.
- She needed him to send more money for a concert.
- She asked him to explain a monthly budget.
- She wanted him to call the dorm administrator to help her get a new roommate.

Sheesh.

It's good and normal for kids to call their parents with questions or advice once they leave the nest, but we should be careful not to solve all their problems for them. Parents should start as early as possible to help their children overcome healthy struggles.

Trauma Defined

Trauma is a serious matter, and it can cause permanent effects. So, how do we allow for struggle without causing trauma? First, we must realize that struggle is not trauma. There's a difference.

Trauma is an emotional response to an event or pattern of events, such as an accident, abuse, natural disasters, neglect, loss, death of a loved one, grief, prolonged pain, etc.

Trauma can be acute, chronic, or complex. Acute trauma can be caused by a specific incident, whereas chronic trauma can result from prolonged or repeated negative events such as domestic violence. Complex trauma is exposure to multiple and varied traumatic events, resulting in a heightened state of stress or fear.

Trauma is a serious issue that many people struggle with daily, resulting in headaches, nightmares, flashbacks, severe anxiety, uncontrollable thoughts, and other mental health issues. If you or anyone you know suffers from trauma, please seek medical or psychiatric help immediately.

Many people have been able to overcome traumatic experiences and turn them into something that helps others heal and grow. We call these people heroes. But there are a lot of other struggles that are healthy struggles that don't cause trauma. For example, exercising, mastering a skill, studying, yardwork, working through a conflict, negotiating, eating the right food, and countless more examples are healthy struggles. These struggles bring capabilities and confidence that allow us to create value for ourselves and others. We will discuss this more in chapter 6.

We're Not Talking Tough Love

Healthy struggle is different from tough love. Although everyone has different definitions, we understand tough love as harsh tactics that are callous or distant in nature. The key is

motivation. Tough love is often motivated by coercion or con-
formity. It's not the healthiest way to raise kids who create
value in the world.

HEALTHY STRUGGLE IS DIFFERENT FROM TOUGH LOVE.

Teach kids how to do hard things. Encourage them to embrace struggle. Give them boundaries and hold them to them, but avoid tough love. This is an unemotional, uncaring form of parenting that can increase feelings of
shame and guilt in your children.

Although it goes without saying, in our work with parents,
sometimes they need to be reminded of unacceptable behavior.
Here's the truth, some of us have had poor examples from our
past. Perhaps we weren't given love, respect, and esteem in a
positive or affirming way. We have a choice. We can perpetuate
the pattern, or we can create a new future for our kids.

Our emotional maturity will cultivate emotional maturity
in our kids. The opposite is also true. In their book, *Hold On To
Your Kids*, Drs. Gabor Maté and Gordon Neufeld give insight
into the factors required for healthy childhood development
and the role of the parent. "The secret of parenting is not in
what a parent does but rather who the parent is to a child."
They explain that a child's brain depends on a parent's more
mature brain to regulate itself. That is why self-regulation in
children has trouble developing through guidance from emotionally immature parents. Here we see why self-regulation
skills are so important to cultivate as parents.

As you might imagine, it's unacceptable to be mean to
kids, harass or make fun of them, or always have them "fend
for themselves." Raising strong kids requires connection and
encouragement in the face of struggle, not unresponsiveness to
their struggles.

By investing the time and energy to read this book, you're
demonstrating your desire for a Value Creation Kid. Because of

this, you have the opportunity to change *someone's* world. When enough parents do this, we can literally change the *entire* world.

Healthy Struggle Is the Answer

In this book, we focus on healthy struggle, but all struggles can be leveraged to create more value in the world. Learn to value struggle. Unfortunately, as a culture, we're moving in a direction where any type of struggle is considered bad.

It takes a couple of cycles of healthy struggle to trust the process. When you do, you come out on the other side, able to create even more value based on the experience where you struggled. Anyone that runs away from a healthy struggle or stays in a state of victimhood because the world didn't produce something that wasn't earned will likely not make the jump to create more value.

Think about instances when you went through difficult times. Afterward, you might have changed your perspective, realizing it was the best thing for you. Yes, it is likely challenging and hard, but you gain power when you gain perspective. The increased struggle equipped you to increase value when you came out the other side. This is trusting the work.

Many kids, and adults for that matter, refuse to take on a project or task if they've never done it before. It can be good to struggle through learning to do something new. When you do, you can create even more value in the world.

* * *

Struggle is required for personal growth, and it is required for adding value to the world. Just ask any athlete, teacher, entrepreneur, or parent. Healthy struggles are simply those challenges in your life that add value to yourself and the world. However, not all struggles are healthy or even necessary. Here are a few examples of unhealthy struggles:

- worrying or experiencing anxiety about things outside of your control
- comparing yourself to others
- trying to live up to unreasonable standards to be accepted by others
- chasing anything that will ultimately leave you empty inside
- getting one more like or heart or follow, or flame on social media (just ask your high schooler what a "flame" is from the new Gas app social media platform)

These types of struggles often kill value rather than create it.

There is one simple way to know which struggles to embrace and which struggles to discard. Ask yourself, "Is this a struggle that will ultimately bring value to myself or others, or not?" If so, then it is a healthy struggle and should be embraced. If not, discard it and move on.

The earlier we start the value-creation journey for kids, the better. Effectively doing this can require a mindset shift for parents around the concepts of Value Creation and the value of healthy struggle. A value-creation mindset makes for a significant change in how you talk about everyday things.

For example, you could ask your child, "Why did you get a B or a C on your report card?" Instead, try asking them, "How do you believe this subject in school will contribute to how you want to create more value in the world?" Or ask, "How much effort should you put into creating that value and why?" Developing a value-creation mindset will significantly change your language and actions over time in all areas of life.

Creating healthy struggles for your kids is a missed opportunity for many families. With the best of intentions, parents want to make life "easier" for their kids, so they don't have to experience the same struggles they did. If life worked this way, our bodies would get stronger by *not* exercising. This is impossible. We can't explain character, wisdom, and experiences to our kids. Just like going to the gym is part of having a strong, healthy body, our kids need to go to the value-creation gym to continually get stronger at creating more value in the world. Getting this right continually elevates self-esteem, purpose, character, personal responsibility, and maturity.

Financial Competency Can Be Fun

Last year, my five-year-old daughter, Reagan, got to take part in her first children's business fair. Her business was Reagan's Flower Power. She spent a week collecting all the old bottles from friends and family. Then, we loaned her forty dollars to buy flowers from the store. After that, she created all the marketing posters and price sheets on her own.

Her inventory included forty-eight vases full of flowers that she sold for five dollars each at the fair. Guess what? She sold out! Two hundred forty dollars in revenue in three hours at the fair. She couldn't believe that so many people wanted her masterpieces. She even got to pay her brother for helping her in the marketing department. Her self-esteem and confidence went through the roof, immediately spilling over into her performance in school and sports.

> If you want to see the full video of how Regan split up the profit from her business, go to GravyStack.com/book.

Financial competency means teaching our kids the art of making and managing money well. Money should be made when material value is created in the home. Most parents skip this step and just start giving their kids an allowance (or free money) to spend, which doesn't connect Value Creation to pay and causes a lack of motivation in the child. Other parents never pay their kids for chores or anything at home, and the kids never make money decisions either. This only delays money decisions for teens when they are out on their own, which is usually costly and has long-lasting effects. We solved this problem in the GravyStack app with our automated Home Gigs process. We will cover this more in the House Rules chapter.

It's worth noting what happens when families use the Home Gigs feature. Within a month of using our system, GravyStack™, kids never ask parents for money again. They simply know how to create it. And they quickly move on to do community gigs to get extra money that gets split among their Save, Spend, and Share accounts.

Parents actually save a lot of money by passing certain expenses to their kids. Families no longer have a negative relationship with money. No more bribery or coercion from parents who feel they have to give in to their kids' requests for money. No more fear that they're buying their kids' love or spoiling them. No more kids pitting mom and dad against each other to get what they want. In fact, kids stop asking for money altogether. When the Value Creation system is set in the home, the parent-child relationships are much richer and deeper. Kids actually report higher levels of self-esteem because they know what they have to do to get the things they need by creating value. This transformation results from integrating healthy struggle at home.

Kids Need Healthy Discipline

Proper discipline goes hand-in-hand with healthy struggle. If you don't think discipline and kids should mix, then this book is probably not for you. We believe the ancient wisdom written by King Solomon holds true, "Train up a child in the way he should go; even when he is old he will not depart from it" (Proverbs 22:6, ESV).

Children need discipline to grow, but like most topics, there are many questions when it comes to discipline.

- Am I doing it too much?
- Is it not enough?
- Is it even working?
- Will they hate me or rebel?
- What type of discipline is best?
- When is it appropriate, and when is it not appropriate?

These are all valid questions that should be addressed. Remember that when you correct a child, you create value for them now and in the future.

We are not going to unpack what discipline is best—spanking, timeouts, soap, the star method, the quarter method—because children are all different, and that is for you as parents to decide for yourselves. What we can do is offer some tips along the way. Remember, the goal is healthy struggles, not trauma. As we outlined previously, there is a significant difference.

The earlier you can focus on training your children in what is expected of them, the better. For example, train them how to speak to you and to each other, how to be a first-time follower, how to be respectful and polite, how to do every chore the right way, how to meet new people, and how to clean the dishes after every meal. The more you focus on training, the less you will need any form of corrective discipline.

One of the families we interviewed to write this book, Chad and Jenise Johnson, gave incredible tips on raising their eleven amazing children. Chad leads "Bootcamps" that include adventures with his younger children. They practice everything, including how to:

- Go to the store and be helpful.
- Listen the first time they are asked.
- Clean the bathroom correctly.
- Pack for a trip.
- Change a tire.
- Tie a tie.
- Shake hands well.

As a result, Chad and Jenise don't have to discipline their kids much, and when they do, it shows them what to train for next. My wife and I have adopted regular Bootcamps with our young kids, and it has worked incredibly well. We will discuss Bootcamps more in chapter four on House Rules.

Always focus on the heart of the child. The goal of discipline is not the punishment but to maintain a deep and loving relationship with your child. A child needs to know that you are focusing on the issue, not on them personally. This is why you should never punish a child out of anger or frustration.

Yelling at a child may feel like an immediate fix, but it can cause psychological damage, including anxiety, low self-esteem, and aggression. It also makes them more susceptible to bullying since their understanding of healthy boundaries and self-respect are skewed. Never say things like:

- Stop being a brat.
- You are naughty.
- Stop being a jerk.
- You are our problem child.

When you tie their identity to their behavior, you cause unhealthy struggle. Older kids worry about this even more as they start to push the boundaries.

Never leave a child feeling as if your love for them is contingent upon their behavior. In our home, we have changed how we discipline our younger kids. If they misbehaved, hit a sibling, or disrespected us, we would immediately spank them and send them to their rooms. This did not maintain a positive relationship with them, and our daughter started becoming bitter. We got some help from the Johnsons, and we changed our process.

The change brought peace and harmony back to our house. As part of our new process:

1. We ask them to go to their room and tell them we will be there in a few minutes.
2. We calm down.
3. We have a conversation with them.

The conversation goes something like this. We ask them, "Do you know why you are being punished?" They are nervous, but they tell us what they did. Then we say, "Yes, thank you for telling the truth." Then we would give them the punishment. If they start to cry, we hug them and ask, "Now what do you say?"

Sometimes it took another round of punishment, but they would eventually say, "Sorry, mommy," or "Sorry, daddy." We immediately hug them and say, "God forgives us, and of course, I forgive you." Then we would always find a way to make it right by having them apologize to a sibling or clean up a mess, etc. Once we agreed on what to do, I would give them a high five, and we would go do it. After the first few times of following this procedure, our children changed their behavior, and our relationship with each of them grew deeper.

Our goal is not to be best friends with our kids. Our goal is to be their parent. If we try to be buddies with our kids, the result will be unhealthy boundaries, an inability to correct negative behavior and long-term respect issues.

> OUR GOAL IS NOT TO BE BEST FRIENDS WITH OUR KIDS. OUR GOAL IS TO BE THEIR PARENT.

If you've never disciplined older kids before, it can be a rough start. When we communicate genuine care, interest, and respect, older kids invite more authority. The more you set healthy boundaries and expectations, the more they will respect and trust you, even if these boundaries differ from those of their friends. Also, never forget to have fun with your kids. This element brings a lightness to the relationship.

We've learned these lessons and many others from older mentor couples. We looked around and found a few couples with incredible adult children. We took them to dinner and brought a notepad. We asked them how they raised their kids, how they disciplined them, set boundaries, and maintained healthy relationships. Parents need help being better parents.

Within the GravyStack app, we've built an entire community of incredible parents who want to raise the best kids possible. We share the best resources for parents to raise financially competent and successful kids, parenting tips for all ages, tax savings, planning, creating healthy environments, etc. Our parents help each other by sharing best practices and tips, asking questions, and supporting one another. This is where I get all my best parenting ideas. Hop over to the GravyStack Parent Elite community, and you'll see what we mean.

Tips for How to Speak to Your Kids

How we speak to our kids is often more important than what we are trying to say. A few well-chosen words and a shift in tone has the power to completely transform a phrase and grow your relationship with your kids rather than strain it.

This is especially important as you help your child navigate through healthy struggles and difficult situations that will stretch them. Parents can be triggered, mad, or sad and still not scream or cry to manipulate, call a child names, threaten them, bring up the past as ammunition, gossip to friends and family, or storm out and give the silent treatment.

As a parent, you can't know everything, and you'll never be perfect. You are not your parents, and you have the opportunity to transform how you interact with your children. Keep the good and throw out the bad. Apologize to your kids if you mess up—it helps them learn. Never criticize your partner in front of your kids; it will teach them to do the same. And don't forget to let your kids hear you praise your partner in front of them often.

Your kids will not care how much you know until they know how much you care. So many parents wonder why their kids don't listen to them or even rebel against them. It starts with a focus on the child's heart, constantly reminding them of how much you value them and the value they bring to the world.

45

Encouraging and thoughtful words show care to our kids, making them trust us more in the future. Play the long game here and delay the gratification if it doesn't connect right away.

When a child is met with uncertainty, pain, or trauma, they inevitably think it's their fault. The voice inside their heads will start to take JABS at them: a voice that Judges, Abandons, Blames, or Shames them. As parents, we can help stop this by helping them process emotions, letting them know they are not at fault (if they aren't), and pouring in love. It is difficult for a child who lives in fear of JABS to be able to create value in the world. But a child who feels loved and free from the JABS can begin being a value-creation detective for themselves and others.

When something doesn't go the way your child wants it to, or they didn't follow the rules for your family, ask them what they learned from the experience that they can use to create more value in the future. It is way more helpful to leverage a bad experience or struggle as a learning experience to create more value for the family and the world. Then, continually look for opportunities to reinforce the value-creation mindset within your kids.

It takes three positive experiences to offset one negative experience with your kids. Your child's brain is wired to focus on negative experiences, so try to avoid negative language.

- I can't believe you!
- Why can't you just do things right?
- Now, there's a mess.

Instead, use positive comments.

- Thank you for being respectful.
- You are a sweet, big sister.
- Thank you for waiting for your turn.

Rather than name-calling or getting angry with them, use value metrics. Here's one that works well. "Oh, I'm sorry you made a mess in your room. Would you please go get me a quarter from your Spend Jar?"

Entitlement comes from a kid thinking they are more important than others or deserve certain privileges ahead of their peers. This usually stems from parents who consistently reinforce the behavior by over-emphasizing physical appearance, buying more than what is necessary for their kids, and bailing them out when they get into trouble. We say things like, "If you help mommy clean the table, I'll give you ice cream." Although well-intentioned, this teaches them that a reward is owed to them when they help someone with something.

It's much easier to say a quick, uncreative command such as, "You made your friend sad. Go say sorry!" Instead, try helping them become aware of the situation. "Your friend looks sad. What do you think you could do to make her feel better?"

Strong-willed kids naturally push back. Set clear expectations and help them feel heard. Don't fall for every argument. Decide your list of non-negotiables. It's best to give them a choice and let them help find the answers. "Since your bedtime is 8:30 p.m., when would you like to do your homework so you have time to do everything you want?"

Dysfunctional homes have family members who hide secrets, use aggression, deny problems, move on as if nothing happened, dismiss issues with no behavior change, and rarely express emotions. Instead, they threaten, shun, withdraw, belittle, and shame.

Instead, try using phrases that remove these issues.

Safety: No matter what happens in your life, everything is figure-out-able.

Responsibility: I value you, and I can't let you hurt people or property.

Trust: I know you will tell me when you're ready.

Love: Your job is not to make me happy. I can handle anything that you tell me.

You can be present but still absent as a parent. Signs of absenteeism include:

- no screen time limits
- refusing to give consequences for negative behavior
- lack of eye contact
- inability to speak honestly

To counter absenteeism, set a goal of spending ten minutes of active quality time with your kids at dinner or during a car ride.

Shame kills self-esteem. A child who is shamed for making mistakes will grow up to be an adult who self-induces shame every time they make a mistake. Ensure your kids know that everyone makes mistakes and is wrong sometimes, and we can use them to learn and grow. When a consequence is called for, it should be delivered with an intent to teach rather than making the child feel bad about him or herself.

You want your kids to make their friendship mistakes, learning mistakes, behavior mistakes, and money mistakes at home with you! If they don't, they will make more costly mistakes when leaving the nest. Making mistakes will help them learn to bounce back after being wrong instead of struggling with embarrassment, ego hits, or defensiveness. And your children will be as honest with you as your reaction to the hard truths they may tell you.

Five key relationship patterns develop as a result of childhood trauma and the parenting antidotes to mitigate them, according to Dr. Nicole LePera:

1. **Critical Partners:** We seek critical partners who attempt to change us and make us work for approval. This comes from their parents, who were harshly critical, and nothing was good enough. *The antidote for this for Acceptance.*

2. **Controlling Partners:** We look for this when we never got the chance to make our own choices, and we want someone who doesn't seek our input to make choices. This stems from harsh disciplinarian parents. *The antidote for this is Autonomy or Agency.*

3. **Fixing Partners:** This person wants power and control, so they tend to find a partner who needs "fixing," enabling, or someone to parent them. This happens when a child is raised by parents who were irresponsible with money, substance abuse, or couldn't keep a job for long. *The antidote for this is Reliability.*

4. **Emotionally Unavailable Partners:** This person is used to not being seen or heard and whose parents were unconcerned or dismissive of the child. They are often most comfortable with a partner who is uninterested in their emotional experience or self-absorbed (like handing out emotional breadcrumbs). *The antidote to this is Being Seen.*

5. **Betraying Partners:** this is a kid who sees a parent betray their partner without changes in behavior. This inauthenticity and lack of respect normalize those behaviors in their children. *The antidote for this is Transparency.*

A child of emotionally immature or unavailable parents often has difficulty connecting to other people. The most common occurrences of this are homes with conflict and distant and unemotional parents. Work to control your aggression or frustrations in front of your kids, regardless of the circumstances. Practice sharing your feelings about your day at dinner with your kids to teach them how to use emotional language themselves.

Children need a safe place for healthy emotional processing when traumatic events occur, like divorce or death. Silence isn't a solution. Your presence and care communicate love and value.

When you mess up, as we all do, you can always try to heal the relationship. For parents of older kids, your kids may be waiting for you to say one of the following statements:

- I didn't give you all the tools that you needed.
- I was overwhelmed, and it reflected in my parenting.
- I was trying to work through my own stuff and didn't know how to raise you while healing.
- I didn't know how to handle your emotions because I didn't know how to handle my own.
- I made mistakes, and they hurt you.
- What can I do now to improve our relationship?

Maybe you wish your parents would have said these statements to you too. The truth is we're all imperfect, and we all had imperfect parents.

Kids of all ages crave hearing these ten responses:

1. I forgive you.
2. I love you no matter what.
3. I'm sorry. I made a mistake.
4. Can we talk about what happened? I want to understand you.
5. Let's pause and talk about this in a bit.
6. I like spending time with you.
7. I'm grateful you are in my life.
8. I don't know. Let's figure it out together.

9. I can see you trying hard, and I'm proud of you.
10. It's okay if we don't agree. Thank you for being honest.

Your relationship with your kids does not end when they turn eighteen. It evolves. If all goes well, the parent moves from protector, provider, and nurturer to coach, guide, and friend. But age is just a number, and many kids turn eighteen and have no idea what it means to be an independent, financially competent, successful, value-creating adult.

There's a viral trend right now called "adulting." It's common among untrained, unprepared young adults who need to learn to grow up. Older parents feel the effects of this trend when their adult kids keep finding their way into their wallets.

The Bank of Mom and Dad continues until the child becomes fully capable of creating value independently. And with all the current statistics, especially now with the majority of young adults at home until twenty-four years old or more, we need to focus on helping kids become independent value-contributors as early as possible.

The secret of the GravyStack Method is to help your kids get on the value-creation journey as early as possible, which in turn speeds up their professional and financial independence. And most importantly, it allows for a deeper and stronger relationship with your children that is unattached to bribery, coercion, or any other negative incentive that comes between you and your kids. That is the healthiest and least traumatic way to raise a child. And that is the focus of the next few chapters.

High-Value Takeaways:

- Struggle is a good thing when leveraged to create more value.
- Discipline does not equal punishment. Focus on the issue, not your children.

- Love for your children is unconditional, not contingent upon their behavior.
- Maintain healthy boundaries and be a loving parent who develops your children to create value in the world.
- Let your kids struggle without jumping in too fast, and use consequences to teach them.
- The more you remove struggle from your kids, the harder it will be later in life for them.
- How you speak to your kids and the tone of your voice matters more than what you are trying to say to them.
- The faster your kids become independent value-creators, the closer and deeper your relationship will be with them.

PART 2

THE GRAVYSTACK METHOD

CHAPTER 3

VALUE CREATION

*Change the way you and your kids think
about the world.*

I n Part 1, we defined the three macro categories of Value Creation: Material, Emotional, and Spiritual. In Part 2, we'll
focus on *WHY* it is so important for children to adopt this language and mindset. It is to continually build stronger intrinsic
motivation within your kids. *Value Creation* is the first building block in The GravyStack Method.

THE GRAVYSTACK METHOD™

Value Creation
House Rules
Financial Competency
Healthy Struggle

When children think and act in terms of Value Creation, it brings more meaning and purpose to their lives. It also makes them more capable and confident. These two qualities are the characteristics of every Value Creation Kid. If either of these qualities is lacking, kids fall into another category. Notice the Value Creation Kid Matrix™ below.

VALUE CREATION
KID MATRIX™

Anxious Self-Doubter	**Value Creation Kid™**
High Capability Low Confidence	High Capability High Confidence
Lazy Victim	**Entitled Taker**
Low Capability Low Confidence	Low Capability High Confidence

CAPABLE

CONFIDENT

The matrix is split into four quadrants, and each quadrant is measured by how capable and confident the child is or is not.

A child with a high capability and a high confidence falls into the Value Creation Kid quadrant in the upper right corner. This kid is powerful, and they have the highest level of personal and professional success.

However, a child with high capability but low confidence is in the Anxious Self-Doubter category. This child is capable of a lot, but they lack the confidence to take action, they second guess their decisions, and they doubt their ability to be a value creator. My sweet wife, Amy, feels like she can fall into this category sometimes. Many of these kids have self-image and self-identity issues, but they also have the most potential to soar as a Value Creation Kid.

On the other hand, if a kid has low capability but high confidence, they may fall into the Entitled Taker category. They are very confident in their self-image, but they may lack the capability to actually create value for others. They may think they deserve more than others or that others owe them something they did not earn. This may lead them to consume or take more than they should. Entitlement comes from the belief that they deserve special treatment or certain privileges that are unmerited. Most toddlers are entitled, but Value Creation Kids are not. And overconfidence leads to arrogance, which is never a sign of a Value Creation Kid.

On the other hand, a child with low capability and low confidence falls into the Lazy Victim quadrant in the lower left corner. This is the opposite of a Value Creation Kid. These kids lack both the motivation and desire to go through any healthy struggle at all. They avoid struggle at all costs, choosing instead to live a life of ease and comfort. In doing so, they miss out on gaining the capability and confidence necessary to create value in the world. And when the world starts to pass them by, they miss out on many of the opportunities of the Value Creation Kid. But instead of taking personal responsibility to begin the growth process, they blame others for their own problems down the road. Few things are harder on parents than a Lazy Victim kid who turns into a resentful adult unwilling to grow up.

FEW THINGS ARE HARDER ON PARENTS THAN A LAZY VICTIM KID WHO TURNS INTO A RESENTFUL ADULT UNWILLING TO GROW UP.

The goal is to help create a kid who is constantly increasing both their capabilities and their confidence to create value in the world. This only comes from healthy struggle. Any other combination produces anxious self-doubters, entitled takers, or lazy victims. And the world has enough of these folks already.

Transformation always begins with healthy struggle. This produces the potential for greater capability and greater confidence. When this takes place, Value Creation can follow. Notice the Value Creation Cycle™ below:

THE VALUE CREATION CYCLE™

The good news is that all kids can become Value Creation Kids no matter where they start. This is a journey, and you, as parents, are their guides. Best value

HEALTHY STRUGGLE PRODUCES CAPABILITY AND CONFIDENCE, WHICH, IN TURN, ALLOW FOR VALUE CREATION.

always wins over the long run. Being on this journey teaches everyone this truth as long as they stay the course. Shortcuts only hurt us in the long run. It's important to appropriately be encouraging, consistent, and patient. All of us, especially our kids, move and learn at different speeds.

Children will always be more motivated when they have some ownership. It can take a little time, but once you get your children to a place where they want to accomplish things that create value in the world, your job becomes much more fulfilling and rewarding. As a parent, this increases freedom, peace, assurance, security, and pride. Imagine how you'll feel. Doing the work to get your children to a place where they are intrinsically motivated to create value is more than worth it.

You will want to expose your children to different ways of creating value to get them started. Tell them what you are doing and why. It's important to let them adjust their course over time to find the best value-creation journey for them. Their journey could be music, which can significantly elevate positive emotional energy in the world. It could be an interest in someday owning a business, which will create jobs and strengthen communities. Your kids may choose to create value in the areas of engineering, medicine, construction, services, etc. Whatever the right value-creation journey is for your child, it is important for it to be theirs and not something forced on them.

Your children have infinite value as human beings. This can never be taken away. Self-worth and Value Creation are two different things. Encourage your kids to ignore chasing value from popularity, social status, social highlight reels, etc. That only leads to a victim mindset and low self-esteem.

Make Value Creation Fun

One of my dear friends is Yu-Kai Chou, the top gamification specialist on earth. He created something called the Octalysis

Framework to help make everything more fun and playful. He has used this strategy with companies like Porsche, Google, Marriott* Hotels, software developers in Ukraine, and many more. He also helped us use these gaming mechanics as we built the GravyStack banking app so that kids could have a blast learning to become financially competent. Remember, kids learn through fun and real-life, healthy struggle.

When I first brought Yu-Kai into GravyStack, he said something profound that the primary goal for us was to create an environment where kids were intrinsically motivated to learn and grow their financial competency. This means integrating four components: epic meaning, empowerment, curiosity, and community.

Extrinsic motivation tactics, like scarcity or avoidance, don't work well if parents have to force, bribe, trick, or coerce their kids into learning about money. Financial competence works only if your kids are intrinsically motivated. The GravyStack app is designed to make learning financial competency fun and rewarding for your kids.

Intrinsic motivation is the carrot on the stick that the kids hold out for themselves. It's also every parent's dream. This is why it is so critical for Value Creation to become intrinsic for children while they are in the household. So let's unpack these intrinsic motivators related to Value Creation.

1. **Epic Meaning:** When a child can tie the value they create in the world to the reason they are on this planet, the drive to create value starts to come from within. As you begin to create more value for yourself and others, you start to identify your gifts, skills, and passions. This is the easiest way for kids to learn about what *calling* they have for their lives. We like to call this "The Sweet Spot," or the intersection of these three things: what you love to do, what you are good at, and what

you see as the biggest needs in the world. Where those meet is a good place to live and work. Once kids begin to dial this in, it becomes an intrinsic driver for them for the rest of their lives. And it all starts with healthy struggles to create value all around you.

2. **Empowerment**: Nothing is more empowering to a teenager than successfully creating material, emotional, and spiritual value for others. Self-esteem is lifted, confidence is raised, and the Value Creation begins to compound over time. They stop worrying about the future or problems in the world or what job they will need to get. Instead, they will be more empowered and motivated to keep creating value for others around them. This, in turn, creates intrinsic and material value for your kids. It becomes their way of changing the world because they have seen it done in real life, and they now believe they can replicate it. I can tell you that the feeling you get as a parent when your kids start to "get it" is like nothing else I have ever felt.

> NOTHING IS MORE EMPOWERING TO A TEENAGER THAN SUCCESSFULLY CREATING MATERIAL, EMOTIONAL, AND SPIRITUAL VALUE FOR OTHERS.

3. **Curiosity**: Curious kids are the fastest at finding ways to create value, and all kids are born curious. The key is to keep the world from beating it out of them. There are so many ways that you can help your kids build their curiosity muscles. Ask great questions around the dinner table or while driving around, take them with you to the grocery store or the bank or on errands, ask your kids why certain things work or how they work (clocks, cars, how food tastes, why certain businesses exist, etc.), or try to find problems that haven't been solved in the

community. Help your kids recognize patterns in the world and try to apply them to their own lives.

4. **Community**: A child that feels a sense of value and belonging in a family, a team, a classroom, or in the community starts to build an internal motivation to create value in the group. This can be an extremely motivating driver for kids to know that they are valuable and contributing members of the community. It takes their focus off themselves and draws them up into something bigger. Spiritual value is created when kids know that they can be of service to the greater group, and the reward they get from it is often the highest driver of intrinsic motivation to create more and more value.

Be intentional about checking in with your kids about how they are creating different types of value for themselves and others. One of the great quotes about this topic comes from James Clear, author of *Atomic Habits*: "What we measure, we improve." Or put in another way, "What you care about should be counted."

The point is this: create a cadence to check in with your kids on each of the three types of Value Creation and celebrate their progress along the journey. These can be daily check-ins about how they are growing and creating value or a weekly family check-in with your kids to see progress and celebrate wins. Here are a few questions to get the conversation going:

1. What was one thing you saw today or this week that you realized you could help with? Anything around the house? What about at school? Sports?

2. What's a problem that you see around the house, at school, in the community, or with your friends? How can you create value for others by solving it?

63

3. Who was one person that you saw that you could help today or this week, and what did you do? Think of one friend and how you can help them or encourage them today.
4. What's one thing that you are struggling with right now, and how can we help?
5. What value did you create today?

When your child begins to create value from intrinsic motivation, their worldview begins to shift. They stop focusing on all the negative outside forces that are beyond their control. They stop fearing that the sky is falling and the world is in chaos. They stop comparing themselves to everyone else's highlight reels on social media. Instead, they focus on what they can control—how they can become stronger and create more value around them.

Imagine a teenager who is impervious to the negative forces at work in their lives from the news, from social media, from bullies, from having to look or talk a certain way to fit in, or from any negative self-talk that can lead to so many mental health issues. This teenager has a greater ability to stay focused on achieving goals and creating positive value in the world.

As you navigate the tension between training proper behavior and building a great relationship with your child, the key is to protect their heart. Your goal is not just to train the behavior but to guide them to become self-motivated to make the right choices. They need to connect with the WHY of a behavior to move them to WANT the behavior because it's best for them.

Learn Your Kid's Language

This is how to steward their heart toward the right behaviors. This is the core of intrinsic motivation. Every child has a unique way of discovering their intrinsic motivation for creating value.

Some will be money-motivated (which is material value) and run in that direction on their own. For money-motivated kids, you can help them build on their intrinsic motivation. Ask questions about how they did it, what they learned, and why they got paid the amount they did.

From there, ask more questions about how they could create more value. Encourage them to test their assumptions, perhaps around what they charge for a service or product. Sometimes the price is too high compared to what others charge, and as a result, few people buy. Sometimes the price is too low, and your children could be leaving money on the table. This can be fun and rewarding as long as you are patient and understand that building on material value (or earning money) will often be slow at first and can ramp up faster over time.

Some kids will not be directly money motivated. All kids have a superpower when it comes to creating value, even if it is unknown and undeveloped. By adopting and regularly using value-creation language with your kids—the first building block in the GravyStack Method— will help them discover their superpower. From there, you can help them build on it.

In doing research for this book, one of the parents described the contrast between his two children. His nineteen-year-old son is highly money-motivated and developed a strong intrinsic motivation to earn more at age fifteen. As a result, he has been doubling the amount of money he earns every year for the past three years. He did this by continually looking for ways to help others in exchange for money.

One evening, the father was sitting around the fire with his son and daughter when his son got a call from a neighbor asking for help moving furniture. His response was, "Absolutely. When do you need me to do it?" The neighbor needed help that day, and he agreed to come straight over after taking care of one other commitment. He didn't even ask what he would be paid to move the furniture.

The next day the son reported that he received four hundred twenty-five dollars to move the furniture, which he split with a friend that he recruited to help. His sister then asked the question, "Why don't these opportunities just happen for me like they do for my brother?" Her father said there is a big difference between the two of them when it comes to taking on jobs to earn money. His son will help anyone that asks, and as a result, more and more people know he is someone they can count on. That is why he regularly gets these kinds of calls. He reminded his daughter that she was asked to organize a neighbor's closet for fifty dollars the week before, and she declined, saying it was not worth her time for only fifty. She responded with, "I see your point."

Simply put, his daughter was not intrinsically motivated to make money the way her brother was. But she had a dormant Value Creation superpower that she hadn't intentionally thought about—creating emotional energy value. I told her father that I observed how his daughter can light up a room when she comes in and interacts with people, more than most people that I have ever met. His response was that she could also take the room down as well if she was not in a great mood. I said this was no surprise, given the power of her emotional energy.

As of the writing of this book, his daughter has taken a job at a high-end resort and is working her way into the event planning part of their business. This requires a lot of interaction with people, where positive emotional energy is highly valued and required to create the best group experiences. My guess is that she will do very well on the job, and who knows, maybe someday, even start her own event planning business.

The point here is that every child (and adult) has a known or unknown superpower when it comes to creating value. You can help your kids by learning their value-creation language. Pointing this out to them will build their courage and confidence.

Help Others and You Will Be Helped

The underlying principle is the more you help others win, the more they will want to help you win. Most people, unfortunately, look at transactions through the lens of "What can I get from this?" which limits the future possibilities for Value Creation.

The more you make every interaction a win-win, the more successful you will be. By creating value, you become invaluable. This doesn't mean giving away all your money, time, and emotional energy without any reward. Of course, entitled takers exist out in the world, but the healthier we get, the faster we can spot these types of people and steer clear of them.

From a very early age, I helped anyone who needed it. If I saw someone on the side of the road with a flat tire or dead car battery, I pulled over to help. As I attained more financial success, I helped causes and friends in need. I used to wonder why so many people wanted to help me. I don't wonder anymore. I went out of my way to help them win, and they did the same for me.

All my efforts to help others didn't turn out so well. Some of my most expensive lessons were helping entitled takers without knowing what they were at first. These were powerful lessons and necessary struggles for me to go through in order to create significantly more value.

I applied these learnings to create more value, and I avoided entitled takers in the future.

I LEVERAGED THESE UNHEALTHY STRUGGLES AND CHOSE TO BECOME BETTER RATHER THAN BITTER.

Value creation is the first building block of the GravyStack Method for a reason. Thinking back to the Value Creation Kid Matrix, it doesn't matter at which quadrant a child starts. By leveraging healthy struggle, any child can move through to a quadrant where he or she is highly capable and highly confident. The journey begins with understanding and unlocking the power of Value Creation.

High-Value Takeaways:

- The great reward of parenting is watching your kids become self-motivated to create more and more value in the world.
- The value-creation lens is the secret weapon for how to view the world.
- Turn your kids into value-creation detectives.
- Your children need to connect the dots to learn how creating value for your family and in the world is the most valuable thing they can do for themselves.
- Kids create the most value when they own the idea.
- Look for signs your kids are creating more value on their own and encourage it.
- Your job as a parent is to create an environment where your kids are intrinsically motivated and empowered to create more value over time.

CHAPTER 4

HOUSE RULES

Do your part and create even more value.

Imagine the power and potential of an entire family intentionally designed to create value. When done right, each family member feels a stronger sense of purpose and belonging. They end up showing up better for the people in their community. The first step in setting up this system is to make sure every family member knows what it means to belong.

Most parents shoot from the hip and hope for the best. When I started applying Value Creation to my life and business, it changed everything. It elevated my mindset, gave me more satisfaction and fulfillment, shifted my career, multiplied my net worth, deepened my relationships, and transformed my marriage with Amy. I became the guy others turned to for help, and I always answered the phone when they called.

Then we began applying Value Creation to our home. We saw our kids quickly become more confident, more capable, and more considerate. There was less conflict in the home. No more bribing them to clean up or do homework. No more trying to buy their love with trinkets or movies, or ice cream. They became more of a joy to be around. They became value-creation detectives.

Just yesterday, as I was leaving the house, my six-year-old Reagan walked up to me and said, "Dad, before you go, is there anything else you need help with?"

Wait a second.

How did my most defiant, independent, strong-willed child just ask me if there was anything else I needed help with? Am I dreaming or living in a fairy tale?

Nope. It's because we had applied the principles in this chapter—House Rules. This is the second building block in the GravyStack Method.

**THE
GRAVYSTACK
METHOD™**

Value Creation
House Rules
Financial Competency
Healthy Struggle

For our family, House Rules begin with our last name.

Your Last Name

Have you ever thought about what it means for your kids to carry your last name? How they should talk, what manners they should have, what you believe to be true about the world, how they should carry themselves, what your family stands for, and how they are to act in social situations. What rituals and habits, and traditions make your family unique? Do you want your kids to carry on your traditions or throw them away?

The fastest way to create spiritual and emotional value in your family is to define what it means to be a member of your family. Write down the ethos of your family, what you stand for, and how you plan to show up in the world. Codify it. Print it out and share it with your kids routinely.

I'll use my family as an example. What does it mean to be a Donnell? Are we polite or rude? Do we clean up or leave messes? Do we quit or push through struggles? What have other families come to expect from the Donnells? How do the Donnells treat other people, and what do we want others to say about the Donnells? What does it mean to marry into the Donnell family (yikes, this one might scare a lot of families away!)? But this is all very important to us, and therefore it's worth writing it out.

In the Donnell family, our last name is important. We come from a long line of kings, leaders, and explorers. Our ancestors trace all the way back to Chief Angus Og in the 14th century, who ruled the MacDonald Clan in Scotland (this could be where some of my William Wallace tendencies come from).

One of our ancestors even cut off his own hand and threw it to the shore of a new island to lay claim to it before the other boat could land first. Our ancestors came to early America to escape religious persecution. Our family ventured across the Oregon Trail in the 1800s, facing incredible odds of survival, and we have their journals from the adventure to prove it.

Our family has many generations of entrepreneurs, politicians, doctors, inventors, pastors, and world leaders. It means something to be a Donnell, and we all feel a strong sense of duty to uphold the family name. It's not an anxious or stressful thing. On the contrary, it brings a deep peace and gives us a sense of belonging.

Because of this, Amy and I created our Donnell Family Credo. This is our Mission, Vision, and Values statement. This is what it means for our kids to be a Donnell, to act like a Donnell, to treat others like Donnells do, and how we choose to create value in the world. Below is a brief description of what each of those elements means so you can begin to create this for your family.

Mission: Your mission is the overarching belief your family has about who you are and what your family stands for. This statement usually begins with "we believe" because it's a core belief that you feel strongly as a family, and if you live it out, you will have the family of your dreams. An example of this is we believe you can be who you want to be.

Here are some questions to ask to find your mission statement:

- What is it we believe more than anything as a family?
- What is it we are really trying to tell ourselves, our family, and the world?
- What is the one belief that, if lived, allows us to create the family and life we dream of?

Vision: Your vision is where you are headed as a family and what you want to be known for. This is what we'd like others to immediately say about us, and it helps us be more committed to who we are becoming as a family. These statements usually start with "we are committed to" as it shows what direction we want to go to take action as a family. An example of this is, We are committed to inspiring and helping other families live the life of their dreams.

Here are some questions to ask to help you:

- What do we want to be known for?
- Where are we headed as a family?
- What impact do we want to have in the world?
- What makes our family unique?

Values: Your values are the behaviors you will create as a family to build a culture in the house to allow you to live your mission and achieve your vision. These are actions that let us love each other better and be more of who we are. Some examples of this are: We love and support each other, we are creators, we are healthy and active, we are a team, we are adventurers, and we do the right thing always.

Here are some questions to help you find your values:

- What is most important to us as a family?
- How do we see ourselves?
- What behaviors do we want to encourage?
- How do we want to treat each other?
- How do we create space for each member of our family?
- How do we allow each member of our family to be who they are?

Based on these three topics, here is what we came up with:

The Donnell Family

Vision:
We believe that God loves us and we are free.

Mission:
We are committed to always supporting each other and creating value for other families.

Values:
Donnells make things better.
Donnells find the good.
Donnells find a way.
Donnells do the right thing.
Donnells are fun and adventurous.

I'd like to thank my good friend Chris Smith, founder of Family Brand, for helping us write our statement. Family Brand is an incredible resource for creating a strong family culture. If you want to learn more, go to familybrand.com.

* * *

Most parents skip this step and just start giving their kids an allowance to spend. Since this is free money, they don't tie money to creating value in the home. In a study conducted by Jumpstart Coalition, they found allowance was linked to a lack of motivation and an aversion to work. Bad idea. Some parents try to pay kids an allowance for weekly chores, which are often missed, and conflict results. The kids end up getting paid anyway. Another bad idea.

Some parents say they never pay their kids at home for anything, chores or otherwise. Their kids are "the good kids" who just get the work done that needs to be done around the house and paying them creates the wrong incentives. This is also a mistake because kids will never have a chance to start making financial decisions at home before they leave the nest. How will they make good purchasing decisions with their own money if they don't have anything to spend? They'll have to learn those lessons after they leave your house when the stakes are higher, and the failures are way more expensive.

What these parents don't realize is they end up paying for many things without letting the kids make those financial decisions. Parents buy toys, souvenirs, games, and clothes. They pay for social outings and trips. They buy all the presents for their friends' birthday parties. Instead, kids could be earning money and paying for themselves. All this adds up to hundreds of dollars a month. You'd be surprised how quickly kids decide not to buy the new Nike® Jordans if they have to use their own hard-earned money to pay for basketball shoes.

In our family, we solved this problem with House Rules.

Your child's closest community is your family. Families can create a tremendous amount of material, emotional, and spiritual value. Everyone in the family should have a job to contribute to the family. This can be keeping their rooms clean and organized, excelling in school, or encouraging other family members. With a value-creation mindset as a foundation, children can learn to love being a strong contributing member of the family.

The House Rules journey is an automated component in the GravyStack app. However, we encourage you to clarify the Three E's:

1. **Expectations**: Clarifying what you expect your kids to do in the home without pay

2. **Expenses**: Listing the expenses that your kids are now in charge of paying for

3. **Extra Pay**: Creating Home Gigs, a list of ways that your kids can earn extra money at home to cover their spending list (we categorize these as Action Gigs and Brain Gigs)

1. Expectations List for Your Children (Roles in the Home)

First, parents decide what chores need to be done for free (we call them Roles in the Home because it's just part of being in the family, and it's your rent!). These are things like brushing their teeth, getting dressed, making their bed, cleaning their room, doing dishes, and taking out the trash. You have to do those things for free to live under our roof, and only then can you start to earn money to pay for your expenses.

Most families never have the conversation about what each family member's role is for the family. Instead, they often have a reactive approach to what does or does not get done in the household. Just talking as a family about the concept of everyone having a role to do for the family can have a profoundly positive impact.

Your children's job for the family is their commitment to Value Creation. This will come in the form of all three types of value; material, emotional, and spiritual. It's hard for our kids to think and act in ways we've never spoken about. No wonder parents and children often get frustrated with each other!

Material Value: We may have given our kids a list of chores, but the underlying purpose and reason is missing if we haven't told them why these are important and how they tie into everyone else's job for the family. Knowing why each child's job for the family is important and how the other family members depend on them can make all the difference.

Your children may not completely understand the power and value of this way of thinking and acting when you first start having the conversations. Be patient and see what happens over time. If you can look back three to six months at any point in time and say your kids have improved in how they do their job for the family, you're on the right track! Remember how long it takes for most adults to understand and apply new things. Our children need time to understand them too.

Emotional Value: Kids can and should contribute positive energy and love within the family culture. Everyone has good days and bad days emotionally. Understanding this and looking for ways to elevate positive emotional energy within the family is a great job for everyone. When one family member is having an off day, we should try not to take it personally. Instead, we should try to lean in and create positive emotional value in an effort to improve the atmosphere.

Spiritual Value: These principles are true for spiritual energy too. This can mean something different for each family. Imagine a family where it's everyone's job to love each other and strengthen the connectedness of the family. When you intentionally talk about these things and incorporate them into each child's job for the family, you have a fantastic foundation. Deep memories and relationships can last a lifetime. It's never too late to start or never too early to begin.

* * *

Expectations are jobs each child does to help make the family strong. The more each child fulfills his or her expectations for the family, the better everyone else can be at theirs. The goal is to create simple and clear expectations so parents don't need to continually follow up and check on what each child agreed to do. In this scenario, parents have more time and energy to do their job better.

Of course, every child and family is unique. However, here is a sample list of expectations for a six- to fourteen-year-old child:

- Keep your room picked up and make your bed each morning
- Brush your teeth in the morning and at night before bed
- Take out the garbage whenever the trash is full
- Clean your dishes after each meal
- Do your homework and give your best effort in school
- Stretch and exercise at least three days a week
- Read at least one book per month
- Feed and clean up after the family pet
- Love and strengthen your relationships with family members
- Do your best to continually improve positive emotional energy within the family

Now consider what would be appropriate for your children, given your family circumstances. It's usually easy to come up with a "job for the family" list for your kids when you are intentional about creating it. Don't worry about getting it perfect on the first pass. It's normal for these expectation lists to evolve over time. It can be helpful for your children to see all family members' jobs for the family so they can see how they fit into the bigger picture and why their job is important.

2. Expense List for Your Children (Spending List)

After the proper expectations are set in the home, the second step is creating a "spend" list of all the things that parents will no longer buy for their kids. This starts with many of the purchases that are "wants" for kids rather than "needs." These can be things like:

- toys
- games
- technology and electronics
- trinkets or souvenirs
- extra clothes on top of the essentials
- extra sporting clothes and equipment
- in-app purchases
- social outings with friends
- trips, concerts, and events
- birthday presents for friends
- for older kids—gas money, car insurance, college savings, and more

What other expenses would you add to this list? There are many more expenses like these to create a healthy struggle for your kids to learn personal responsibility at home.

Each family will be different in what they assign to their kids and when, and we suggest starting with a few expenses and steadily moving up as your kids begin to earn more extra pay with Gigs. Parents can begin assigning these expenses one by one to their kids starting as early as ages 6-8. By the time they get their driver's license, this entire list should be passed on to your kids. If kids don't start making these financial decisions at home, including some small money mistakes that you can all learn from, they will end up making bigger money mistakes later on in life without you. And the Bank of Mom and Dad will just keep rollin' throughout their twenties. Most importantly, parents can now use this extra money they save to pay their kids to do Home Gigs around the house. We will discuss how to create and pay for Home Gigs in the next section.

The list of things you will buy for your kids will be the life necessities and the fun experiences you want for your family. The rest will be up to them. And if you're ever out and about and they forget to bring cash or their GravyStack debit card, you can float them cash to pay you back when you get home. Or you can just remind them that it's their responsibility to have their own money on hand before you leave, and they will never forget again.

The spend list teaches your children the value of money and the work required to earn it. This also helps develop their decision-making muscles. Most kids can't have everything they want. This process not only teaches them to prioritize their wants, but it also gets them to understand the value of each thing they do end up buying. When the value of money means something to your children, they will think twice about not overpaying and product quality.

As with every building block in the GravyStack Method, it's important to be intentional with your children. When creating and implementing the spend list with your kids, ask for their input and discuss why you're doing it. This is for their understanding and ownership in the short run and creates huge benefits when they become an adult. You never want to change the rules without helping your children connect the dots to why you are doing it. Of course, make these conversations age appropriate.

3. Extra Pay for Your Children (Action Gigs or Brain Gigs)

This final step of House Rules is extra pay or the extra ways that kids can earn money around the house and in the community to pay their expenses. We call these Gigs, and they can be done at home or in the community. The goal for Home Gigs and Community Gigs is to make them simple, clear, and fun for children and parents alike. Since the goal is for kids to have fun and learn to make and manage their own money, we try to avoid using words like "chores" or "work" to keep them excited. The GravyStack app provides a list of over fifty-five Home Gigs for kids to do around the house to earn money, based on their age. They can also see a list of Community Gigs to choose from in their community or with friends and family to earn extra pay. These paid projects teach kids the value of money based on the work required to earn it. Gigs allow kids to earn their own money and spend it on their wants and needs as they choose.

There are two types of gigs that kids can do to earn money at home or in their community. One type of gig is done by using your hands and feet to make money, and we call those Action Gigs. The other type of gig is making money by using your brain, and we call those Brain Gigs.

Action Gigs: Action Gigs are paid jobs that require working with your hands and feet in order to accomplish the task. These jobs usually require some sort of physical labor, though they can still be a lot of fun for kids and teens. This list can include cleaning the garage, doing yard work, pumping tires, washing windows, making meals, cleaning bathrooms, mopping or sweeping, organizing books, assembling furniture, washing cars, or even helping siblings with homework. The list varies depending on the home. They can be valued as low as one dollar and up to twenty to thirty dollars, depending on how much the parents want to pay their kids monthly and the level of autonomy they want their kids to have.

These gigs are set to automatically repeat daily, weekly, monthly, or as one-off projects. We even send you a GravyStack email once a week with the new checklist to print off and put on the fridge. Kids receive a weekly paycheck to their bank account in less than sixty seconds for all the gigs they have completed. For a full list of these Home Gigs, you can go to

GravyStack.com/book and begin the process of Value Creation in your home, starting today.

Brain Gigs: Brain gigs are paid gigs that require you to think with your brain more than using your physical labor. These can be articles to read and respond to, extra educational videos beyond school, books, Ted talks to watch and write down the lessons learned, mindsets to master, writing up a contract, not eating sugar for a week, or even researching a topic for mom and dad to make a decision. A good brain gig always requires some sort of feedback from the child about what they learned and how they want to apply it to their life. Design brain gigs to increase your children's capability, which in turn makes them more capable and confident to create value in the world.

Brain gigs are tasks and challenges that kids can read, write or watch to learn about a specific topic or practical skill that is important to you as their parents but also to your close relatives or friends. Grandparents and relatives are the perfect people to give paid brain gigs to your children. Two of our close friends, Tom and Georgia Barnett, have been paying $10-20 to their grandkids each time they finish a specific Ted Talk or PragerU video and write up a summary of what they learned. They have paid thousands of dollars to their grandkids, and they couldn't be happier about helping pass on what they feel to be life's most important information to the next generation. It sure beats just giving them money for their birthdays and hoping for the best. Many of our friends have done the same using books or articles, or videos that they believe to be critical for their kids or grandkids at their specific stage of life.

Brain gigs are meant to be educational challenges for kids that are above and beyond their normal homework for school. Finishing homework on time with excellence should be the expectation in your home, and you should not pay for it. But why would we want you or your relatives to pay your kids to complete these brain gigs? The reason is that your kids need to learn that they can use their brains to gain special knowledge to create value for others. Many of the highest-paying jobs require more brain work than grunt work, and most of the jobs of the future will require more brains than brawn. Just ask any lawyer, financial planner, engineer, technologist, consultant, executive, or a whole host of other careers that use their brains instead of their muscles to make money and help others. Kids need to learn this valuable lesson early.

In my long career, I've spoken with thousands of high school seniors about financial competency. I always ask two questions:

- Would you feel better if you were dependent on someone else to pay your bills?
- Would you feel better if you earned enough to pay your own way and not be reliant on anyone else financially?

Guess how they answer? The students answered 100 percent of the time that they would feel better if they were financially self-reliant.

While financial competency is foundational to your kids being successful in adulthood, there are many other Brain Gig opportunities for you to choose from. We encourage you to use your judgment to select categories that will help your kids be more successful adults. They can choose life skills, mindsets, learning a foreign language, and many more.

* * *

Both Action Gigs and Brain Gigs are designed to give children the capabilities and confidence to thrive as adults. What's the result?

As we mentioned in chapter 2, within a month of using the GravyStack app, most kids never ask their parents for money again. They simply know how to create it. And they quickly move on to do community gigs to make extra money that gets split into their Save, Spend, and Share accounts.

WITHIN A MONTH OF USING THE GRAVYSTACK APP, MOST KIDS NEVER ASK THEIR PARENTS FOR MONEY AGAIN.

Parents find they no longer have a negative relationship to money with their kids. No more bribery or coercion, no more begging for money all the time, no more fear that they are buying their kids' love or spoiling them, and the relationships are actually deeper because the system is set for their kids to create value instead of having so much gray area. Kids actually report higher levels of self-esteem because they know what they have to do to get the things they need by creating value. This is the power of healthy struggle and removing the wrong incentives in the home.

For a sample list, Action Gigs and Brain Gigs, you can go to gravystack.com/book.

Boot Camps Help Reinforce House Rules

While your kids and teens are still at home, you have a special window of time to "show them the ropes" and teach all the practical skills they need in life. Kids are very hands-on in their learning, and they need you to actively explain and model the correct behaviors, skills, tasks, gigs, and all sorts of other essential skills for life outside the home.

Most parents want to connect with their kids, mentor them, and show them something valuable—anything other than having them numb out watching a show. But where do you begin? Parents need ideas in those moments. We've come to find out that boot camps can help.

Earlier in the book, I mentioned Chad and Jenise Johnson, parents of eleven incredible kids. One of their most effective training tools is called Daddy (or Mommy) boot camps. This is a special time with mom or dad, either before or after dinner or on the weekends, to learn something together. The skill can be simple or complex, depending upon the child's age, but the point is to train them on day-to-day tasks and skills. With young kids, it starts small, like learning to tie your shoes, cleaning your plate after dinner and stacking it in the dishwasher, or how to make your bed properly.

With a little thought, we soon realize how many things we do for our kids daily—tasks they should be doing themselves. That's where boot camps come in. We can set expectations for them on how to:

- properly clean up their rooms
- do laundry
- clean the toilets
- care for pets
- act when guests come over
- buy groceries
- how to properly pack and unpack from family trips
- making purchasing decisions

The lessons are endless and just require a little time and repetition.

Most disciplinary and parental struggle comes from a lack of training. The more you practice the correct skills and behaviors, the more the children will model them in the future. This is the fastest way to create a self-managing family and relieve yourself of many of the things that bother you. Kids are much more capable than we give them credit for, but many parents enable their children. If you make their lunch every day, they will grow to expect it. If you clear their plates, they will devalue the effort required to eat a meal. If you pay for everything, money won't matter to them. If you buy their clothes, pick out their clothes, pick up their dirty clothes, wash their clothes, fold their clothes, and put away their clothes, then you are their butler. Do yourself a huge favor and begin as early as possible.

Any parent of older children will admit that almost every skill that their kids do today could have been learned a few years earlier, and it would have saved them years of unnecessary stress and work. You have enough to do! And the longer you wait to give them boot camps, the harder it will be to unlearn undesirable behaviors down the line.

In order to help you in this process, we have curated a list of ideas from several trusted families. Here's a list, categorized by age for convenience:

Ages 0-5

- daily affirmations, goal setting, verse or wisdom meditation, dinner devotions/reflections
- First Friday Family Party Night (planned out every month)
- how to go to the grocery store
- how to travel in an airport
- how to unpack from a trip
- how to greet people and shake hands, look in the eye
- Super-quick Clean-up After Meal Party (SCAMP)
- how to clean the house
- creating a kid business to sell $100 of product
- how to tie your shoelaces
- how to clean the bathroom
- how to organize a closet
- navigating the kitchen: basic cooking, using a stove and oven, meal prep, deep cleaning, tiny habits in the kitchen

- how to throw, catch, or kick a ball
- marshmallow/Cookie game to teach delayed gratification
- institute the penny or quarter program at home to earn pennies for projects or good deeds to earn things
- begin cooking a meal for the family (and involve them!)
- how to make your bed
- never be a victim mindset coaching
- gratitude letters and focusing on the positive things
- teaching Integrity: Do The Right Thing Even When No One Is Watching
- how to be giving and generous and give as a family

Ages 6-9

- cut off allowance, set up list of Home Gigs or money
- how to tie a tie
- how to change a tire
- how to wash and fold laundry
- how to build things—a birdhouse, playground, house, and more.
- outdoor survival, make fire, roughing it
- gamily presentations on topics to learn public speaking
- erite down fifteen affirmations for thirty days in a row and memorize them
- how to create a calendar; time management for the day
- search to solve a problem around the house, hunt to create value
- empathy conversation and how to resolve conflict in the family
- how to set and reach a goal
- teach delayed gratification; buy first stocks together
- how to be a great friend and make great friends at school
- hard fitness challenges after dinner and on weekends
- oversee meal prep, cleaning stoves, chopping food

- chivalry: opening doors and proper eating etiquette
- how to ask good questions and be interested in others and visitors to your home
- how to tie ten different knots
- basic first aid, how to handle a cold and the flu, calling 911, what if you see someone unconscious or sibling choking, things to watch out for (electricity near water, outlets, pool, fires, sharp edges, poisonous fluids, don't go into traffic in drivers' blind spots, earthquakes and tornadoes, or intruders)
- basic hygiene, shaving, and puberty preparation
- negotiating skills and how to get to Yes with others
- Family Culture, Mission Statement, and 5 Core Values (review and live them together)
- learning forgiveness techniques
- body language for listening, confidence, empathy, and love
- begin bargain hunting, clipping coupons for groceries, and canceling monthly subscriptions. give 50 percent of the savings to your kids.
- get your own savings account and debit card for spending

Ages 10-13

- set up 50 percent matching for car or college savings plan, and let them find ways to make money
- how to do taxes, find all State/Federal taxes
- navigate how to get home on a trip
- cold plunges together for mental toughness
- learning calendars and time management
- how to hunt and clean an animal or fish
- how to prepare for a job interview and get any job
- how to change a tire, change the oil, basic car maintenance
- online safety and security, protecting your data, etc.

- how to treat servers and tip correctly
- minor home maintenance and improvements: changing air filters, turning off water, basic plumbing and electrical, unclogging a toilet, painting a wall, changing a lightbulb
- how to have an abundance vs. scarcity mindset, find their passions
- do a difficult adventure to build courage and bravery (rock climb, hike, etc.)
- participate in the family quarterly service project in the community, like a soup kitchen
- how to give and accept feedback or criticism, and how to be unoffendable
- find gigs to do in your community going door-to-door (and do at least ten jobs)

Ages 14-18

- start a business together, make them fund at least half the price of a car or college
- how to write a great resume and cover letter
- applying for college or a career

High-Value Takeaways:

- Every family member should be clear on what their job for the family is and how they create value for the family.
- Teach the value of money through your expectations, expenses, and extra pay.
- Your family is the testing ground for your kids to be successful in life.
- Find the right balance of action gigs and brain gigs.
- Conduct weekly boot camps at home.

CHAPTER 5

FINANCIAL COMPETENCY

Leverage the Right Tools for a Self-Reliant Life.

The third building block of the GravyStack Method centers around helping our children gain Financial Competency as early in life as possible.

THE GRAVYSTACK METHOD™

Value Creation
House Rules
Financial Competency
Healthy Struggle

We say "financial competency" instead of "financial literacy" because our focus is much more on helping people learn practical money skills that are useful in the real world. Literacy is a more academic word that sounds hypothetical rather than practical. And it sounds like boring homework. You can't read money like you would read a book; learning money is a skill, a capability, and expertise gained only by experiencing it.

Financial competency is the art of making and managing money well. And money is made when material value is created.

So why is financial competency so critical to a value-creation kid? Because money is simply a tool that measures value—nothing more and nothing less. Money is the most tangible reward for creating material value in the world, and it's hard to fake it. Many people go wrong when they put money on too high of a pedestal and allow it to run their lives and steal their joy. Other people are tricked into undervaluing or villainizing money, and in doing so, they end up with more financial struggles and bitterness in the long run. By leveraging the GravyStack Method, a Value Creation Kid understands money is simply a tool to measure value, and they learn how to master this tool in order to have a productive and fulfilled life.

* * *

There are many problems when it comes to teaching financial education. For starters, schools have a very hard time teaching kids about money because it is a personal thing, and it can only be learned in the real world. At best, schools teach it only through hypothetical homework, which doesn't work. Secondly, banks don't offer help because most kids don't have money, so they simply opt out of the conversation. Thirdly, parents are not sure what to teach their kids, and they're unsure if their kids will listen. This is why 76 percent of twenty-five-year-olds fail a basic financial literacy exam. Teaching kids about money requires a unique approach, which is why we created GravyStack.

Kids learn best with two primary elements: fun and real-life experience. Without play, kids are forced into learning through power or coercion, and learning feels more like homework. Without real-life experiences, everything is theoretical, and kids can't apply their learning to something concrete that sticks in their long-term memory. It begs an important question: how much of what kids are learning nowadays is boring, repetitive, assembly-line homework that doesn't have to do with real life? The more we can urge educators to focus on real-world training in hard skills, soft skills, professions, taxes, budgeting, investing, and life skills, kids will have a better chance to be successful.

KIDS LEARN BEST WITH
TWO PRIMARY ELEMENTS:
FUN AND REAL-LIFE
EXPERIENCE.

Financial competency cannot be learned as a theory, and you can't teach it through more homework and tests. It has to be experienced by real kids making real money and learning to save, invest, and spend that money in the real world. Healthy struggle with financial competency in the real world is what makes kids capable, confident value-creation machines. While this book addresses financial competency at the individual level, the biggest positive impact will be visible when schools incorporate a value-creation mindset into the K-12 curriculum.

Many states have passed financial education standards, but the jury is still out if they will be effective. We will be giving out the GravyStack program to schools upon request, but parents can always do more to influence school boards to move in this direction. If the Value Creation Kid movement spreads, we will have a significantly higher percentage of kids reaching adulthood who are financially competent and as financially independent as they want to be. We believe this could fix much of the $2 trillion student debt crisis in our country.

Here's an example of one of the levels of the GravyStack game called Savings Beach. It has ten missions to teach savings that are a combination of mini-games of wants and needs, fun quiz games, real-life challenges to cancel subscriptions, find coupons for the next visit to the grocery store, and help kids automatically save a percentage of their money in their Save Jar in the GravyStack bank account.

* * *

We want to solve problems before they start. This is why we focus our attention on teaching our kids at home while they are young because it's often harder to unlearn something than it is to learn it.

When we started GravyStack, we surveyed a thousand families. Not only did parents not know what to do, but the kids' responses shocked us! We asked the kids some questions about what they were learning or not learning, how prepared they felt to enter the real world, and the life skills required for success.

And what did they say? The kids didn't actually want to talk about money in the home because it was the topic that most commonly caused arguments between their parents.

Obviously, parents don't fight about sex in front of their kids, but they do express conflict about money.

- We can't afford that this month!
- You forgot to pay this bill.
- How are we going to pay for that?
- There's no money for that!
- Do you know how hard I worked to pay for that?
- Money doesn't grow on trees.

Chances are your parents said some of these statements. Kids see their parents stressed over money more than anything else, and it makes them run the other way. The kids feel that at least they have the necessary food, shelter, and clothes to survive, so they would rather not discuss money for fear that it brings up more issues at home. As a result, many kids expressed that they would rather deal with money later on when they are out on their own. Such an environment is not conducive for kids to learn about creating value. In fact, only a small percentage of kids are hardwired from the womb to find ways to make money without any parental guidance or support. The rest of our children need our help as parents to learn to make and manage money wisely, and it all starts with the way you talk about money around your kids.

* * *

Creating a home environment that is conducive to financial competency begins by learning to master the top seven money categories. These categories are listed below, followed by a brief explanation and practical applications for each one:

1. Earn
2. Save
3. Spend
4. Share
5. Invest
6. Protect
7. Borrow

As a note to parents, each of these money traits has its own level with ten missions in the GravyStack app. We also have additional levels that address Value Creation and the skills and traits required for financial competency. However, we did not include those extra levels on this list because they have each been addressed elsewhere in this book.

1. Earn

Since we have devoted much of the Value Creation and House Rules chapters to helping kids learn how to earn money at home and in their community, we will only briefly discuss the matter in this section. But we wanted to highlight this again because financial education is impossible unless money is first earned before it is spent. Why is this true? Because you cannot learn financial competency by spending someone else's money. You cannot learn the true value of something when it is given to you for free. A child needs to earn money first before they save, spend, share, or invest it. This is why allowance usually fails. This is why it is very hard to teach financial literacy in schools. And it is also why our government spending is so out of whack—it's easy to spend other people's money, especially when if you fail, you can just print more money and go further into debt. That does not create value.

Money is earned as a result of creating material value for others. It is made from solving problems for profit. The better you get at honing your skills to create material value for others, the greater the potential for financial reward. The *Value Creation Kid* quickly learns to find problems in the world around them they can help solve. They don't just complain about the problems like many other people do; instead, they see them as opportunities to create value. They find something that other people need or want, and then they find a way to help get it for them. This is how value is created.

There are many ways to earn money. You can earn money by performing a valuable task for someone, called a job or a gig (we call them Home Gigs and Community Gigs). You can earn money by creating a product or service that fills a want or need in your community, like selling candles or babysitting. This is what many entrepreneurs do. You can also make money when you buy something cheaper and sell it at a higher price later on down the road. Buying things that grow in value are called assets. People buy houses, stocks, businesses, art, baseball cards, or many other assets that grow in value over time.

Try to help your kids earn money from each of these types of income streams. Give them a ton of Action Gigs and Brain Gigs at home for extra pay. Help them find a few products they may want to sell in the community or at a local Children's Business Fair. Give them ideas of services to provide in the neighborhood. Help them buy their first stock, or for teenagers, find a real estate property to work on buying together. Go to a yard sale and look up the price of whatever you find to see if it is worth more money online, and learn to make money off of the difference. Gary V is a huge fan of this type of earning, and we even have games in the Earn level of GravyStack to help kids profit at their local yard sale.

For a full list of over 135 ideas to help your kids create their first home business, go to gravystack.com/book.

Earning money sets the table for you to be able to learn the rest of the categories of financial competency listed below. Most people focus only on spending money to teach financial literacy, and that is a mistake. Your kids will be much better off learning to earn money first.

2. Save

The simplest way to save money is to set it aside and then don't touch it. Saving comes before spending and sharing.

> *Do not save what is left after spending;*
> *spend what is left after saving.*
> —Warren Buffett

This isn't a popular opinion in today's world, where instant gratification and buying what you want immediately is the cool thing to do. However, the key to financial competency is to make decisions now that set you up for success later. Do the hard things now so you have greater reward in the future. Live like no one else today, so you can live like no one else tomorrow.

The key to saving early in life is learning delayed gratification. Simply put, delayed gratification is choosing *not* to get something now so that you *can* get something better later. This is actually one of the core pieces of healthy struggle—voluntarily doing something hard in order to have a greater benefit later.

Kids who practice delayed gratification tend to have better life outcomes, as was discovered in the famous 1972 Marshmallow Study at Stanford University by psychologist Walter Mischel. In the first study, there were thirty-two children ages three to five years old. They were offered one marshmallow immediately or two marshmallows if they waited for fifteen minutes in a room alone. The participants were followed for the next several decades. The study revealed that the children who waited for the greater reward had more successful outcomes in SAT scores, college graduate rates, body mass index, and many other success indicators.

But there was more to these studies on delayed gratification that we found interesting. The original assumption in the experiment was that having the kids focus on the single marshmallow for fifteen minutes would motivate them to gain a large reward after the time limit. But what they found was that kids would do anything to not look at the marshmallow. They would cover their eyes or rest their heads in their hands. They invented games with their hands and feet to pass the time. They sang to themselves or talked to themselves. One kid even fell asleep!

Those who stared too long at the marshmallow were more likely to eat it. This showed that just focusing solely on the reward can actually cause a decrease in delayed gratification. But by not thinking about the reward, you can get through the struggle more easily. This is why we believe that successful habits are the most important trait of a Value Creation Kid.

Every action you take is a vote for the
person you want to become.

—James Clear

* * *

One great tip is to practice putting your money in the Save, Spend, and Share accounts (or jars). Each GravyStack account comes with three sub-accounts called Save, Spend, and Share. Every time a kid makes a dollar, he or she automatically splits it up between those three jars based on the percentage of their money that they want to go in there. The Save money is put away for the future (used for investing), the Share money is for helping others, and the Spend money is for your living expenses (wants and needs). Every kid and their parents decide on the correct percentage of money to go into each account. Then whenever money comes in, we create an animated GIF to show kids how the money is split into each jar and where the money goes if they spend it. This is our way of turning monthly statements into something fun!

A recommended model for saving is to use the 70/20/10 rule.

- 70 percent of your income is for spending.
- 20 percent of your income is for saving.
- 10 percent of your income is for sharing.

Because spending happens over time, you have to first make sure the savings and sharing money is pulled out first. Then you can spend the rest.

In our family, my dad flipped the formula for me. It changed my thinking and made me a millionaire in my twenties. He said, "Scott, most people spend 70 percent and only save 20 percent, but in our family, the secret is to work hard to be able to save 70 percent and spend 20 percent. That's the key to long-term wealth. So the goal is to save seven out of every ten dollars and do your best to keep that rule until your investments, not your paycheck, pay for your lifestyle."

SCOTT DONNELL AND LEE BENSON

I realized if my monthly living expenses were three thousand dollars, then I wanted to try my best to make ten thousand dollars a month. Now that I have been living that way for decades, the money that is saved and invested is paying for our living expenses.

Saving money gives you cash confidence and a safety net when the future is unknown. Without saving money, you will have nothing left for emergencies that come up. In the GravyStack game, there is a level called the "Emergency Expense Water Balloon Fight" where the players have to dodge water balloons thrown by one of the henchmen. This character is a rhino, and to stay dry, they have to identify the emergency expenses inside of each water balloon. Things like a broken window, a cavity, a broken leg, a faulty air conditioner, or a grandparent who needs help.

Kids learn the cost of over thirty emergency expenses as they beat the game and earn Grits. It shows them why it's so critical to save early and often. We suggest having at least six months of living expenses in your savings account, so if an emergency expense comes up, you've got it covered.

Here are a few great tips to learn about saving with your kids:

- Learn the difference between wants and needs and write down ten of each.
- Make sure you are spending at least twice as much on needs instead of wants.
- Set up your three jars at home.
- Write down at least twenty emergency expenses to prepare for.
- Cancel a subscription with your kids.
- Eat at home instead of going out and calculate the savings.
- Pay your kids 50 percent of the savings from grocery coupons they find.

Each of these savings lessons is a game in the GravyStack app.

3. Spend

Spending money is easy, but the Value Creation Kid learns to spend money wisely. The secret to wealth is to spend less than you make. Try to spend only on things you need rather than the things that you want. You can't just make more money to fix bad spending habits because, eventually, you will go broke. Many famous people have made millions of dollars, and they spend it all on cars and houses and jewelry, and other useless wants. When you spend more than what you are making, you go into debt. Remember, it's very difficult to get out of debt. (We will cover this in the borrow section.)

Value Creation Kids spend only what is budgeted to be spent. They buy what is needed first, and then they prioritize what they want after that.

There are countless ways a Value Creation Kid learns to spend wisely. They don't allow their identity to be wrapped up in what they wear, having the newest things, or how they look. They know how to find coupons and deals, how to buy in bulk, and how to use generic products when it makes sense. They don't have to buy the fanciest thing in order to be successful. Many people try to look cool by showing off expensive things, but secretly they are broke. True wealth is usually quieter, and your money looks better in your bank account than on your feet.

One of the toughest spending habits to teach to our kids is the monthly budget. This is because kids don't have normal expenses in their everyday life. They live in their parent's house, and most of the expenses are paid for by their parents. Because most children lack the motivation to create a budget, the key here is to gamify this experience and find a way to attach a budget to their future careers.

Inside the GravyStack game, while the kids and teens are moving through the Spend Forest, they enter a Tree House Job Fair. Their goal is to help a dozen of the animated characters find the perfect job and then live on the monthly income from their job. They have to place each character in the right job based on their education and interests, which are always different. Then they create a budget from that job's income. Kids earn Grits, or points, in the game by how well they do and how happy they make the characters. We've even created a leaderboard to inject a little competitive play against their friends.

In the game, we use national statistics to create a database of the top 185 types of jobs in America and the average income from each of those jobs. As the kids play a particular mission, they are actually learning all the different types of careers they could have and the income from those careers. As they help the characters find the perfect job and then live on that budget, they are learning valuable lessons about spending in the process.

For example, if one of the GravyStack characters has a four-year degree and loves math, spreadsheets, and managing money, the kids would look through the list and offer certain jobs that might fit them, such as finance or accounting. Let's say that they find the perfect job, and it pays $5,100 per month to start. The next step is to help the person live on that amount each month. After allocating an automatic 10 percent of the income to savings and paying off any educational loans, the kids help the character decide how to spend the rest on sub-categories. Each sub-category has multiple tiers based on what they can afford:

- **Housing:** Do you want to buy a house, rent, rent with a friend (half the cost), or live with your parents?
- **Transportation:** Will you take the bus, rent a car, buy a used car, buy a new practical car, or a luxury car?

- **Food:** Will you eat basic, average, organic, or gourmet food?
- **Communication:** Will you have a cellphone, internet, high or low data plan, or all of them?
- **Extras:** Will you spend money on extras such as going out to eat, having a pet, taking trips, attending concerts, buying clothes, etc.?

After children pass this level, they are prompted to find three careers that interest them and make their own budget based on the income from those jobs. Then they are challenged (for more Grits) to sit with their parents and go through some of the expenses to see what their family spends on housing, transportation, food, and communications. This has proven extremely valuable to kids and parents so far, and we challenge you to do the same for your kids. For more resources and a simple budgeting calculator for families, go to GravyStack.com/book.

Note: Many parents aren't comfortable sharing their annual income with their kids. They are hesitant talking about their net worth, their debt amounts, and even how much money is set aside for their kids' education and future (if any at all). You don't have to share any of this information with your kids when discussing a monthly budget.

Simply adding up what your family spends on food or housing each month is plenty to get your kids to begin understanding a budget and setting their own goals for later in life. Our advice is to tell your kids as much as you feel comfortable sharing (whether good or bad) to add value to their future because real examples are what help kids become the most financially competent. Lastly, kids are not fragile. You won't scare your kids or make them love you any less by sharing mistakes as well as successes in your own life. We trust you to be appropriate in these matters, and this is why we created the GravyStack Parent Elite community in the app to discuss these issues together and share best practices.

Another tool to help your kids learn to spend money wisely is the free Money Motto Quiz in the first level of the GravyStack app. Kids and teenagers play a game that helps them find their core money motto, how to leverage it, and where blind spots could pop up. They might lean towards being a Status Shopper, Practical Consumer, Analytical Buyer, or Emotional Spender. The app not only rewards them with Grits, but it also gives them tips for how to use their spending type in life, and how to protect against the downsides of that money motto. Another great quiz on this topic to learn spending is called The Money Mammal Quiz by John Lanza.

4. Share

We define sharing as the personal giving of what you own to someone else without requiring anything in return. We like to use the word "share" with kids and teens because they can identify with it more than "giving" or "charity." Sharing is more than just giving away money. Kids learn to share their toys or food with their friends before they start giving money to feed someone in a foreign country. Sharing is best taught by helping your kids first share with a friend or family member, then someone in their neighborhood or community, then someone nationally or globally. It's a process.

You cannot give your kids money for free and then ask them to give your money away. That's not charity; that's them allocating your capital. For them to learn to be generous, your kids need to take a portion of their hard-earned money and willingly give it away. This is exactly why we have a Save,

Spend, and Share account for each kid in GravyStack. They have to make money first and then learn to part with it to create value for others.

In the GravyStack app, we have created a Spend List of a dozen expenses that parents should be passing on to their kids so that the kids can learn financial habits at home, such as planning, trade-offs, and exchange of value (see House Rules in chapter 4).

A kid has to know how many Home Gigs they have to do in order to earn enough money to buy sports equipment. It often makes them decide on the cheaper version, and they will appreciate it more. One of my favorite expenses on the Expense List is birthday presents for your kids' friends. How many times have you paid for a gift for your kids' friend for their birthday party? You wrapped it, you got the card, you had your kid sign it, and you even put it in the car because they forgot. Then they bring it to the party and throw it on the table and forget all about it. Half of the time, your kids don't even know what the gift was!

This is not sharing, and it is not generosity. But what if your kids had to use their hard-earned money and choose a great present for their friend, buy it, and help wrap it? When your kid goes to the party, they will be so proud of that present that they will go right up to the kid and give them the gift and say, "I got this for you myself. Open it!" The joy they get from this type of giving is powerful and unforgettable, and you, as a parent, have set them up for life to be more thoughtful in how they share and give to the people in their lives.

Sharing is a muscle that's built over time. And sharing can only be taught from a mindset of abundance rather than scarcity. You have to believe that tomorrow will be better than today. You have to believe that there's more than enough to go around. You have to believe that you are a value creator.

Last month, Rick Karjalainen, my youth pastor, passed away after a long battle with cancer. Rick was one of the most formative people in my life,

SHARING IS A MUSCLE
THAT'S BUILT OVER TIME.
AND SHARING CAN
ONLY BE TAUGHT FROM A
MINDSET OF ABUNDANCE
RATHER THAN SCARCITY.

and he taught me more about sharing and generosity than anyone. Almost every month between the ages of twelve to sixteen, Rick would take my friends and me to feed the homeless in downtown Seattle, Washington. We would pack an entire trailer full of tuna fish sandwiches, cowboy coffee, cookies, fruit, and clothes. We would drive two hours to Occidental Park, nicknamed Jurassic Park because of all the drugs and violence, and we would set up shop all night long. It was always cold and always a struggle for us, but it was nothing compared to what these people were going through.

We fed between 300–400 homeless people there throughout the night, learning their names, giving out clothes, praying for them, connecting them to the local shelter, and giving toys to anyone with kids. One time, I even took off my own socks for an older man who needed them after we had run out. I could not be more grateful for that time and for Rick, who invested so much to teach us the value of sharing. You make a living by what you get, but you make a life by what you give. Much of how my family gives today from our charitable trust is because of that time. Thank you, Rick.

Sharing and generosity come from a place of gratitude and thankfulness for what you have, combined with an understanding that you can use what you have to create value for someone else. This is the true superpower of a Value Creation Kid. Instead of doubting themselves, playing the victim, or being an entitled kid who takes from everyone else, the Value Creation Kid has the confidence and capability to create so much value for themselves and others that it overflows into the lives of everyone they meet. He or she is a joy to be around.

If you want to begin the process of helping your kids learn to share, start local and move out. First, help them find one family member or friend to help. Then find someone to help in your school or community. Then find a local charity that they care about and volunteer on a Saturday afternoon. Don't just give money to them—get your hands dirty and try to get as close to the front lines as possible. After that, think about a national or global charity to support or even plan a family mission trip. We have an entire level of games in GravyStack to help kids learn about their favorite types of charities, learn about nonprofits, interview a generous person in their life, and even connect their Share account to a charity to start giving.

5. Invest

Investing is taking your resources, whether time or money, and dedicating them to something that produces a return later on down the road. All business owners, the stock market, the global economy, the banking system, and every millionaire or billionaire on earth will tell you investing is the key to success. And the true secret for kids is to do it early and often, even if it only starts with a few dollars a day.

> INVESTING IS TAKING YOUR RESOURCES, WHETHER TIME OR MONEY, AND DEDICATING THEM TO SOMETHING THAT PRODUCES A RETURN LATER ON DOWN THE ROAD.

If you take just five dollars per day and automatically invest it into a diversified portfolio, which is a fancy word for putting money into lots of different types of stocks and bonds, and you don't touch it, you'll be a millionaire in two decades. This is usually called the Coffee Millionaire principle: if you invest the price of a coffee each day, you'll be a millionaire in 20 years.

However, my good friend Caleb owns a bunch of coffee shops, and he doesn't like that example. In fact, he took his love for coffee and built a business now worth many millions of dollars. So maybe you could replace the word "coffee" with carpooling or eating out or ice cream or Diet Coke* or extra clothes, or anything else you can stop buying and use the money to invest. The key is to invest that money automatically first and before paying other expenses.

You can invest both your time and your money to create more value for your future. For a child, it's important to teach them their time is actually more valuable than money. If you choose to invest your time wisely in the things that create the most value, you will be way ahead.

Time and Money

Teach your kids to invest their time in learning about how to create value for themselves and others instead of in video games, social media, or Netflix. The Brain Gigs feature in the GravyStack app is designed for this exact purpose. You and your extended family can give your kids educational challenges to earn extra cash. They can read an article, watch a Ted Talk, read about certain topics, and interact with them for pay. They need to learn you don't just earn money with physical labor but by using your brain to think.

Some of the best advice I ever received was The 3% Rule. I took 3 percent of my annual income and invested it into my personal development and my network. I started small by reading books and finding great mentors. Then I paid for courses and classes on business and investing. Then I went to events. Then I joined masterminds with other high-level entre-preneurs. Then I created my own communities, which is why we now have the GravyStack Parent Elite community to help the best parents get even better.

I learned from the best in the world and applied the knowledge to grow my businesses, my family, my skills, and my net worth. And almost all my closest friends came from these experiences. I have now invested millions into my personal development, and the value it has created for myself and those around me has been exponential. The saying is true: your network becomes your net worth!

Have you ever audited the time you invest in yourself on productive things versus the time you waste on unproductive things? The average adult spends eight-and-a-half hours on their phone every day. The average teenager spends six hours on just social media every day! You'd be surprised to find out how much time is spent on non-value-producing or mindless activities.

Don't forget resting and playing together can be time well invested. How are you investing in your kids during the short time they are in your home? Remember, 93 percent of all the time you will get with your kids will happen before they are eighteen years old and leave the nest. Invest well.

Delayed gratification regarding time *and* money are both central components of investing. You must be able to delay the reward of something today to create more value in the future. The Value Creation Kid invests time and money in their future because they know they'll reap a reward down the line.

Compounding Interest

Compounding interest is often called the Eighth Wonder of the World. When you invest ten dollars for a 10 percent return, you will have eleven dollars next year, and you will make $1.10 the following year. This is called appreciation. Over time, that money multiplies, and in 10-15 years, it has doubled! Then all that extra money will also be making 10 percent, and you are now living on passive income.

If a teenager starts investing in the stock market, they will be way ahead of anyone who starts investing later on in life. In fact, someone in their twenties will have to start investing twice as much per month as a teenager to get the same amount of money by the time they are sixty-five years old. And someone in their thirties will have to invest four times as much, and so on. The time value of money is one of the great secrets for a Value Creation Kid.

> IF A TEENAGER STARTS INVESTING IN THE STOCK MARKET, THEY WILL BE WAY AHEAD OF ANYONE WHO STARTS INVESTING LATER ON IN LIFE.

Did you know that a 529 Education Savings Account is a tax-deductible investment that you can make each year to save for your child's future education? Thousands of dollars can be invested tax-free, and it can grow each year for your kids. Did you also know that if your child chooses not to go to college (which many parents are starting to consider), the leftover money in that account just rolls over into a tax-free Roth IRA account?

Have you ever wondered why Gen Z is the least invested generation in history by a wide margin, even with all the new trading and investing platforms? This is worrisome. I believe for many. This is because they don't trust investing in the market.

They have seen multiple recessions, global pandemics, crypto crashes, and countless lies on social media. Some of the fastest-growing social media influencers for teens right now are crypto traders, day traders, and get-rich-quick scammers. Our kids have more access to information than ever before, but it's less valuable information. This is where your practical wisdom can come in handy. Teach your kids these simple investing disciplines while they are with you. Let them make real decisions with their money and even fail a little bit. It's much better to learn these lessons in a safe environment with you rather than after they leave the house. Later on, the stakes are much higher, and the debt is more expensive.

Teach your kids to invest in themselves, in good friends, in practical skills that create value, in real estate, and in the stock market. We have many games in GravyStack to help. We even give kids an investment account in our Save Jar to begin the journey while they're young. They play games with the characters in GravyStack to learn delayed gratification and compounding interest, as well as risk and reward. They even learn to find products and services around the house that are public stocks. We help them learn about the stock and what makes a good stock. And they actually invest a small amount in the winners!

6. Protect

When we say protect, we are talking about cybersecurity and insurance, two of the most important ways a child can learn to be safe in our world today. Online security is rarely taught to kids, especially when teaching financial competency. Yet we know it's a crucial skill for our kids to learn in an ever-increasing technological world.

There are more threats to our data, our information, and our safety than ever before. There are scary people in the world who want to hurt our kids. We cannot hide our kids from this reality. Instead, we must prepare them.

In many cases, children and teenagers are more tech-savvy than their parents. Just ask any parent whose five-year-old made an in-app purchase on their iPad without the parent even knowing it. However, young people lack the intuition and wisdom to know when they may be getting into trouble or giving away too much information.

The goal here is to always keep the conversation open and let the topic of safety evolve over time. Kids are receiving their first smartphone earlier and earlier, with more than 70 percent of eleven-year-old kids now having their own smartphone. We have chosen not to give our kids their own phones until well after puberty. We have strict rules in our house about limiting screen time and putting phones in the basket at dinner time for the night. We also don't allow tech inside the bedroom. Even though the GravyStack app may be considered good tech for parents, in our house, we allow only a limited amount of play time per day per kid, and the child doesn't need their own device to use it.

Online Protection

A Value Creation Kid knows how to safeguard themselves from risk and danger, both online and in the real world. They know how to protect themselves and their information from online threats and unknown problems that may come up. We have an entire level of games teaching kids and teens to protect themselves online. Here are the main issues that we address:

- **Passwords**: We want kids to know how important it is to keep your password strong and safe. "Passwords are like underwear: don't let people see them, change them often, and never share them with a stranger." One of the challenges in the game is to have them download a VPN password manager to keep their passwords safe and generate new passwords every few months.
- **Data:** We teach kids all the types of data that they have that are valuable to someone else and why those people may want to hack them to get this information. We teach them why it's important not to give their data to anyone without approval from their parents. We teach

the most valuable data that can be stolen and the price of that data to others, such as addresses, emails, cell numbers, health data, social security numbers, etc.

- **Permanence:** What they say online remains there forever. It's there for all to see, even their parents, future spouses and kids, future employers, and everyone else. We teach them about cyberbullying and the problems that arise and to use care when talking to others online. And we especially teach them to never give out private photos of themselves to anyone, no matter who they think that person is. Their risky photos could be screenshotted and used for blackmail.

- **Catfishing:** You never know who is on the other end of a social media account or an email, or even a text. A person could make you think they are a friend or a pretty girl at school, but they could be a sixty-year-old guy in his basement tricking you.

- **No Judgment:** Encourage your kids to tell you (or another adult) if someone tricks them, blackmails them online, or tries to extort them. This is the biggest way that a predator or dangerous person will harm your kids—they will create a fake account as a young, beautiful person and trick them into giving photos or information, and use it to blackmail them into meeting in person or giving other information. "I'll send this to your parents and everyone you know unless you meet me at this location tomorrow at 4 pm by yourself" is a common ruse. Kids must know that there will never be any judgment if they tell an adult when they are in a scary or embarrassing situation.

- **Hackers and trackers:** We teach kids the top ten ways they can be hacked, scammed, or tricked online so that they can be aware of potential dangers in the future.

Cybersecurity is one of the most undervalued skills we can teach our children at home. And with new advances in machine learning, artificial intelligence, and quantum computing, the need to protect your online reputation has never been higher. The stakes are high, and you usually don't know about the problem until it's too late. The key is to keep an open conversation going with your kids, and our goal in GravyStack is to set up those conversations. You should also consider teaching this to their grandparents.

Offline Protection

We also know kids must learn the importance of insurance to protect their health, their family, and their belongings from unknown danger. GravyStack families know how to plan ahead and protect themselves from emergencies. It's good to have an emergency fund and six months of living expenses in case there's an issue that comes up. It is important to teach your kids the value of health insurance, car insurance, home insurance, life insurance, and other protection from risk and unforeseen circumstances.

The last area of protection that kids can be made aware of is saving money on taxes. Some taxes are important for our country, and other taxes are bad for our country. There is much debate on this issue, and because we want this book to be for all parents regardless of their views on taxes, we choose to keep our personal opinions out of it.

Our goal is to unite parents together with the goal of raising successful kids who create value in the world. But even our government doesn't want its people to pay unnecessary taxes. The tax code has been created as proof. The truth is there are many legal ways for families to save on taxes and prepare for their future, and much of that is covered in our GravyStack Parent Elite program in the app.

It's important for kids to understand the taxes they will have to pay, such as wage tax, local tax, sales tax, state tax, federal tax, consumption tax, death tax, and many others. The more they know, the more they will be prepared. If we had known about all the tax deductions and strategies available to us, we could have protected ourselves from paying thousands of dollars of unnecessary taxes over the years. This would have allowed us to share even more with those who need help the most.

We care about the protection and safety of every child. Whenever a family joins GravyStack, our company donates funds to anti-trafficking organizations that focus on teaching online security and helping save millions of kids from predators and traffickers around the world.

7. Borrow

Borrowing money is using someone else's money for a period of time, usually to purchase something for yourself, with the promise to pay them back later on, plus a little more. That little more is called interest. People can borrow money to go to school or buy a house. The higher the interest rate on the money that you borrow, the more you will owe them after you pay them back the initial amount.

Money can be borrowed from family or friends, banks, financiers, or payday loans, often called loan sharks. If you borrow money, you usually have to personally guarantee you will pay them back with either your own money or something else you own, like your house or your car. That is called collateral. If you can't pay back the money, you go into default and maybe even bankruptcy, which stays on your credit record forever.

It's one thing to borrow a pencil from somebody in your math class. It's another thing altogether to go into debt. The question about borrowing money is not how much to borrow but whether you should do it at all. There is nothing more controversial or more debated in the financial world than debt.

Some people say it's a great way to build wealth. Others say it is terrible and to avoid it at all costs.

THE QUESTION ABOUT BORROWING MONEY IS NOT HOW MUCH TO BORROW BUT WHETHER YOU SHOULD DO IT AT ALL.

We have a personal example of this in GravyStack. We have some influential friends from both the debt-good world and the debt-bad world who strongly disagree on this topic. Two of the more prominent people are the folks from the Dave Ramsey organization and Grant Cardone's group.

Dave Ramsey is anti-debt. He believes you should do whatever you can to avoid going into debt. Pay it off if you have the money, starting with the highest interest rate debt first. He agrees with what Thomas Jefferson said, "Never spend your money before you have it."

Ramsey is against credit card debt because the interest rates on that debt are as high as 24 percent, and people who use credit cards instead of debit cards or cash are likely to spend 30 percent more money without realizing it. He created Financial Peace University, which is a great course, and many of our friends and employees have taken these courses over the years. The confidence you get from living debt-free will allow you to take more risks and grow more wealth in the future.

Dave makes some very good points. Credit card companies make billions of dollars a year off credit card debt. Many people in our world today are pinned down by so much debt that they are barely able to cover the interest payments. The borrower is always a slave to the lender, and every time you borrow money, you could be robbing your future self.

On the other hand, Grant Cardone is a real-estate mogul who talks about leveraging as much as you can to buy assets because it is the fastest way to grow your wealth. He has raised billions of dollars to buy large real-estate properties and other businesses that have appreciated in value over time. This has allowed him to grow his equity and net worth exponentially. He believes cash in your account is a waste of space and that you should be putting all your cash into either real estate or maybe even the stock market. Using other people's money is the best way to grow your income and net worth.

Grant also makes some really good points. Many of our close friends have used debt at different times in their lives to grow their businesses and build homes, and it has worked out more than it has not. When it works out, it's awesome. When it doesn't, it's devastating.

I'm sure both camps would change some of our words to clarify their arguments. We did our best to paraphrase. But the point is smart people fall on different sides of this borrowing equation.

The question we want to answer is how do we teach our kids about borrowing money? Both parties agree debt is a serious matter that you have to be careful about. But when it comes to kids, each parent will have to make this decision on their own based on their own experiences and goals for their kids.

One of the best ways to teach your kids to borrow is to draw up a contract with your kids to loan them money to buy something they want. You can be as favorable or heavy-handed as you want, but set the terms up front:

- What interest rate will you charge?
- How long do they have to pay it off?
- What is their collateral if they don't pay it off?
- What sort of payments will they make along the way?

Let them feel the pressure of borrowing and help them calculate how many Home Gigs and Community Gigs they will have to do to pay off the loan. You can go as deep as you want with this exercise and let your kids learn as much as they want in the process. We have seen some pretty hilarious assets being put up for collateral, such as bikes, stuffed animals, trophies, and even doing laundry for a month. Just don't allow them to put up a sibling!

Our views on this issue are not set in stone, but we want to take the middle ground on the issue. We like the idea of steering clear of debt as much as you can, especially as you are learning to become financially competent. Credit card debt is an absolute No. However, if your teens do have a credit card to build their credit score, bills should be paid monthly, without fail.

If your kids are college bound, start saving and investing early and set parameters for how the money can be used and how much your kids have to earn on their own. The 50/50 rule is always good here. Student loans are tricky because you don't know what the child will major in and how much money they will earn from the resulting job to pay off the loan quickly. It's painful to see a twenty-four-year-old saddled with debt. Oftentimes graduates don't realize how much of their paycheck will be eaten up by the cost of their degree.

The point here is for kids to learn that there is always a cost to borrowing money, and people today are way too flippant with the debt they take on to live their lives today instead of living for tomorrow. Debt is a serious matter and should only be considered for assets that will appreciate in value. A home, for instance, is likely to appreciate in value over time, though its value could go down in the short term. Make sure to try and cover as large of a down payment as you feel comfortable so that monthly payments are easy to cover even if circumstances change. A business venture may also require some debt, but it can easily go sideways and cause a whole world of problems, especially with a personal guarantee. You need to plan for every scenario before going into it.

Value Creation Kids know how to use money in their favor. They know how to treat it with respect, but not to value the money itself. They know that the best money comes from creating material value, and other ways of getting money are unpredictable.

* * *

Financial competency turns math into something practical for everyday life. Our teenage children are required to learn complex mathematical equations in calculus, algebra, and geometry. But how will algebra ever help them to create a monthly budget? How will calculus help them understand taxes or investments or why credit card debt is such a bad idea? Education must first be rooted in practical application. Only then can you move into complexity.

Our favorite type of math might surprise you. This type of math is about learning to calculate the future value of what you decide to do right now. Calculating the future impact of your decisions today is the most important math that anyone can learn. Value Creation Kids learn to weigh their actions and decisions today based on how much value they will create in the future.

CALCULATING THE FUTURE IMPACT OF YOUR DECISIONS TODAY IS THE MOST IMPORTANT MATH THAT ANYONE CAN LEARN.

- How will this video game create value for my future?
- How will this school project impact my future, and how can I do it in such a way that it will add value to me later on?

- Do my friends today align with who I want to be in the future?
- What Home Gigs do I need to do today to make enough money to go to the movies with my friends next week?

You don't have to be a master of financial competency to start the conversation and make progress. Each of us earns money based on someone else paying us for the value they see in our best efforts in delivering a product or service. Try asking your kids these questions:

- Why do you think it is important to earn money?
- What things can you think of doing to earn money?
- What things can you think of doing to create even more value to earn more money over time?

Let them struggle a bit to discover how they can earn money and ways to earn more by creating value for others. Schedule a value-creation conversation with your kids every month to see how their thinking and actions can evolve. This should be an ongoing process in your home as the results become exponential over time.

The key is starting the conversation and always searching for better ways to create value. If you have these conversations regularly, your kids will continue to discover better ways to create more value for themselves and others.

Ask your kids the same questions about why it is important to save. How does saving create better options for their future? Your kids will feel great about themselves when they save for and buy bigger ticket items on their own. Talk about how savings can eventually generate additional income. If your kids save regularly and for long enough, their savings can potentially generate all the income they will need to maintain their lifestyle at some point in their adult life.

Teach your kids the value of spending less than they earn. We've all heard the expression that *money is burning a hole in my pocket*. In other words, I have it, and therefore I need to spend it. This is a great topic to have the conversation about living within your means and spending money wisely.

- What does living within your means and spending money wisely mean for your family?
- How can you improve how you leverage the way your family members spend money to create even more value for your family?
- Start the conversation, and over time, you will always discover a better way.

Investing money needs more attention in most families. What is the difference between sound investing and gambling? Sound investing is putting money into anything with a solid history of providing a return on that investment that is predictable and within your acceptable risk tolerance. Gambling is the opposite. In these types of investments, you are taking a chance on something without a solid history of providing a predictable return, and the odds are stacked against you.

Take the time to learn something about the difference between investing, speculating, and gambling. Having these conversations as a family will help your kids avoid making poor investment choices when they become adults. Again, consistently and appropriately have the conversation, and your conversations will deepen over time.

Sharing or giving money to others or causes can make us feel good, but also, it may not have the desired effect we are looking for. There are many charities in the world. Millions of them, actually. And they all have a stated purpose for how the world is better because of the work they do. Giving money to a charity without confirming what they do with your donation (money) can mean your donation will be wasted. Many charities do not effectively use donations to make a difference in the world that they claim. Sharing should both make you feel good and make a positive difference in the world that is important to you.

Giving money to help friends can really help them in an emergency. It can also keep them from experiencing their own healthy struggles to create value in the world and may actually make them worse off. If you or your kids want to give money to friends or family members, ask the question, "Is this money supporting their own healthy struggles in order for them to create more value over time or causing them to avoid learning and growing on their own?" We all want to help and it can feel really good to do so. The essential question to ask is "will my assistance help in the way I want it to?"

For sure, money is not more important than emotional energy or love. It is, however, foundational to support basic needs, save for emergencies, and support causes that are important to you. For your kids, having money could mean they can buy a toy or game they want. Or, they could save it to buy their first car or build a college fund.

Having money allows us to focus intensely on creating more emotional and spiritual value in the world. By teaching your kids financial competency at an early age, you show them how to connect those dots to create material value. The GravyStack app can assist you in making it easy by gamifying learning financial competency and applying what they learn through experience. Another great benefit is that the GravyStack app makes it easy for you, the parent. The goal here is to make learning easy and fun for both you and your kids.

Financial competency and how to apply those understandings to creating material value is core to being able to create all types of value in the world. For example, many nonprofit organizations will say their primary drive can't be about the money. It has to be about the impact. The impact could be things such as saving animals, teaching kids in underdeveloped parts of the world, overcoming drug addiction, etc. Without money, you can't pay for the impact. In nonprofits that truly create more value in the world, impact and money are inextricably linked. One can't grow without the other. This is true for everyone because we need the financial resources required to live the lifestyle we want as adults.

The same principle applies to for-profit businesses. Lately, we hear talk that doing business can't be about profit. It has to be about purpose. The same rules apply here that do for nonprofits. If you want to have a positive impact on the world through a business, you need profits to pay for it. Again, purpose and profits are linked.

It's important to develop a healthy relationship with money. Any money you save is just the sum of your accumulated best efforts someone else valued enough to pay for. As your best efforts create more value over time, as seen by others, you will have the opportunity to earn more. Money is a tool and a resource for you and your kids to leverage to support your family and community as well as all the wonderful things you want to do in the world.

> ANY MONEY YOU SAVE IS JUST THE SUM OF YOUR ACCUMULATED BEST EFFORTS SOMEONE ELSE VALUED ENOUGH TO PAY FOR.

High-Value Takeaways:

- Financial competency is more powerful and practical than financial literacy.
- Kids learn money best by having fun and through real-world experiences.
- The key to wealth is spending less than you make.

- Money is just one of the outcomes of creating material value.
- Pay yourself first, then save, then share, then buy needs, then buy wants.
- Debt is a serious topic and should be considered only for things that grow in value.
- Protect yourself and your family against online threats—you never truly know who you are talking to online or who is listening.
- Go to GravyStack.com/go to begin training your children to become financially competent today.

CHAPTER 6

HEALTHY STRUGGLE

Making it easier now often makes it harder later.

Congratulations! You've made it to the fourth and final component of the GravyStack Method—Healthy Struggle.

THE GRAVYSTACK METHOD™

Value Creation
House Rules
Financial Competency
Healthy Struggle

With the best of intentions, many parents have gone out of their way to give their kids what they never had as children. They want to create a better, easier, and more painless environment for their children to grow in.

This sounds like a good thing, right? It depends. It comes down to what you believe your job is as a parent while preparing your kids for adulthood. Is it to make your children's lives easier and for them to have more stuff than you had? Or is it to develop your kids to be self-sufficient, confident, and productive value-creating adults?

What You're Up Against

Unfortunately, the idea of kids using healthy struggles to create value in the world is systematically beaten out of them from an early age. They are trained to escape struggle from the beginning. Children spend less time outside exploring the world because parents are more worried about the dangers. They teach the kids to be scared of other people who might harm them. As a result, children meet fewer people. They don't know their neighbors, and they are increasingly less able to find ways to help others.

Kids spend more time on screens that numb their brains, which keeps them from being curious about the world around them. We bribe them with sugar or iPads˚ to keep them compliant and quiet. Teenagers stare at phones that hijack their amygdala and get them addicted to social media apps that constantly provide them with a dopamine rush from swiping up. They're more anxious and depressed because they compare their lives to the fake highlight reels of others.

They see news that polarizes people and scares them about the future. Scarcity is pumped into their brains, and they think there is not enough to go around. They're taught capitalism is a broken and greedy system and that they're helpless victims. None of these things teaches kids to create value in the world around them.

Many schools have become assembly lines that focus on making sure kids follow the common core curriculum to pass the tests, get good grades, go to college, and get a job somewhere. Schools want to crank out good employees who do what they're told. We're taught to be quiet, not to make a mistake, do what we're told, and not to collaborate with others. We're taught there's only one right answer to the problem and usually only one way to get to that answer.

In the real world, none of this produces a successful adult!

We need to synergize and collaborate with others, learn to ask hard questions, negotiate and persuade, problem-solve, and learn to think for ourselves. In the real world, there's an infinite number of possible answers to reach a goal or outcome. Memorization is not education—neither is money. Learning to create value in the world is education. All teachers care, and they want to put kids first. And the best way to do that is to teach them life skills like financial competency, collaboration, and how our government works so they can make better decisions as adults to improve the conditions for all of us to work, live, learn, and play.

Parenting Extremes

Parents respond to these negative pressures in different ways. Some try to micromanage every aspect of their child's life, systematically removing freedom and curiosity from the child as they develop. This is called Helicopter Parenting. Children raised in these circumstances tend to have stronger symptoms of anxiety and depression as they struggle under the constant pressures and scrutiny created by their parents. Helicopter Parents operate out of fear, removing healthy struggles from their children by over-manufacturing their environment. As a result, they create unhealthy emotional struggles in their children.

On the other end of the spectrum is a new wave of parents who use Free Range Parenting. This is a form of parenting that allows kids to function independently and with limited supervision. The goal is to help kids build confidence and gain freedom gradually as they navigate the natural world around them.

Parents stop worrying about or hovering over their kids, and they let their kids learn their own consequences and take their own risks. While this can help kids learn more creativity and problem-solving, it can also have downsides. It is a good thing to help your kids learn independence. But be careful of raising your kids to have a profound distrust of authority structures. Some critics even see this form of parenting as too permissive, uninvolved, or even a form of neglect. We believe balance is best.

Regardless of where you fall on the spectrum, be intentional about giving your kids both structure and freedom. When we focus on helping kids create value in the world around them, many of these parenting styles will fall into the background. When we set up a system for our children to become value-creation detectives, they can leverage a good structure for creating value and the freedom and creativity to do it.

Making the drama go away short term for your children or buying their love can be bad long term. Pushing the "easy button" too many times can have lasting negative effects. Accomplishing challenging tasks builds self-esteem and requires a certain amount of healthy struggle. What is challenging for one child may not be for another, depending on their age and capability. You will likely not get it perfect every time, but the goal is to design the right amount of healthy struggle for your kids to take the next step in their value-creation journey.

> WHEN WE FOCUS ON HELPING KIDS CREATE VALUE IN THE WORLD AROUND THEM, MANY OF THESE PARENTING STYLES WILL FALL INTO THE BACKGROUND.

Launching your child into adulthood at eighteen able to think critically, be financially competent, be as financially independent as they choose to be, and contribute to strengthening your family and the communities they engage with is a clear goal. If we make it too easy on our children, it may take them an additional five to ten years past eighteen years old to be productive adults who add material, emotional, and spiritual value to your family and the world.

When intentionally designing for healthy struggle, think about it in three stages: observation, practice, and building.

Observation: The observation stage is where you intentionally expose your kids to an environment where value-creation language is being regularly used and applied. This way, they can see that it is part of your family culture and benefits other family members.

Practice: The practice stage is where you add to the value-creation language by exposing your kids to tools so they can practice creating value. It may be a little clunky at first for your kids. This is a great example of healthy struggle and kids will go at different speeds in effectively applying the tools and practices.

Building: The building stage is where your kids have demonstrated they can create value on their own and are starting to build on it with intrinsic motivation. Once your kids get on the right value-creation track, it will be difficult for them to ever get off. This is a great thing to strengthen the family.

Many parents distance their children from healthy struggles without realizing it. Have you ever heard or said these words as a parent? I want my kids to:

- have all the things that I never had growing up
- never have to deal with what I had to deal with as a kid
- have all the opportunities that I never had

Parents mean well when they say this, but they forget these experiences are what made them into who they are today. Most wealthy parents who protect their kids from struggle are actually separating their kids from becoming financially competent themselves. This is why 90 percent of generational wealth transfer is squandered or lost within just two generations.

This doesn't mean we pass on our negative experiences of anxiety, abuse, fear, anger, neglect, abandonment, or any other trauma to our kids. But parents often trade in healthy struggle for ease as they raise their kids.

Protecting kids from healthy struggles only removes or delays the value-creation journey. How often do we save our kids from the consequences of their poor choices? It starts when they are young and we clean up their messes. Out of expediency (or exhaustion), we ignore when they disobey or disrespect us. We give in and get them the ice cream or toy or extra TV time, even though they did exactly the opposite of what we asked.

We run back to school the moment we find out that they forgot their lunch or PE clothes, or homework. When they tell us they have a school project due the next morning at 7 PM the night before, we scramble to help them complete it. We argued with the referee or the coach if the call was bad or if our kid was subbed out too early. We do their laundry until they leave for college, and they end up buying dozens of $1 t-shirts at the thrift store, and they bring home a month of dirty laundry for every visit (or maybe that's just what I did). We are trying to help our children, but it does not teach them personal responsibility.

Parents argue with the teacher to get their kids an A. They overcorrect and fix their kids' homework, making the kid feel like they can "mail it in" because mom will just fix it. They fight with the coach to make sure their kid gets more playing time or makes the starting lineup. They pay for everything for their kids, and they never let their kids earn money at home to start making financial decisions (and mistakes) early. Then they wonder why The National Bank of Mom and Dad continues until the child is 28 years old.

I personally know a mom who got the Driver's Ed teacher fired when her kid failed the driving test! How does that help a child learn to solve their own problems and create value in the world? It doesn't.

Participation trophies are fine at young ages when you don't keep score, and the focus is on basic skills, teamwork, and having fun. But once you introduce scoring, competitive drive, and work ethic in sports, then only the winners should get the trophy. And if you lose, it's a great learning opportunity to feel the sting of defeat, pick yourself up, and keep going. These are the perfect opportunities as parents to encourage your kids and make sure they know you love them regardless. You can inspire them to dig in and keep trying.

Every kid should feel what it's like to win and lose in as many ways as possible if they want to learn to push through struggle and create value in the real world. Giving a trophy to the kid who lost the game is like spitting in their face—they don't even want it! There are no participation trophies when you don't get into the college you wanted, or when you screw up the job interview, or can't make a mortgage payment. In life, you can win, or you can learn. Both are okay.

One great way to begin the value-creation journey is having your kids find a need to fill in the home and in their community. At GravyStack, we have a list of over one hundred ways that kids can make money in their community to begin creating value. Washing cars, walking dogs, raking leaves, mowing lawns, babysitting, taking out the trash, putting up Christmas lights, etc. For a full list of these ideas, go to GravyStack. com/book.

Case Study: Using Gigs as a Family

Chad Willardson is a friend of ours who helped create GravyStack. Chad is a wealth manager and author of the best-selling book *Smart Not Spoiled: The 7 Money Skills Kids Must Master Before Leaving the Nest.* He's also the founder and president of PACIFIC CAPITAL, a fiduciary family office serving high-net-worth entrepreneurs. Chad and his wife Amber married in San Diego, CA, in 2001 and have five children: McKinley, Pierce, Sterling, Bentley, and Beckham. Each of the five kids has a predictable way to make money outside the home.

McKinley Willardson is a basketball rockstar sponsored by the Air Jordan brand at age 17. She decided to use her talents and skills to earn her own money by starting her own sports business as a trainer. She hosts basketball training, group clinics, and individual coaching sessions for kids ages six to fourteen. This takes place in her own backyard. At times, she was earning over $130/hour. She earned and saved enough money to pay for her own mission trip to Africa in the summer of 2022.

Pierce Willardson is a fifteen-year-old sophomore in high school. He started his own community business for painting address signs on the curbs. The business initially began with the summer holiday rush of July 4th. He rode his bike around neighborhoods, looking to see which addresses were faded and which used to have symbols like the American flag. He made his own "potential client list" in his phone's Notes app. Next, he bought his supplies with his birthday money and began selling door-to-door. He earned close to $80 an hour plus tips on a good day, and he loves the customer feedback when they come out to the street to admire the finished product.

Sterling Willardson is twelve and has a great love for animals. While the Wilardsons are busy with five kids and traveling with ten sports teams, they don't have time for pets. Sterling decided to turn his love of animals into a way to earn money, a dog-walking business. He used Canva.com to create flyers and went door-to-door asking who would love their dog to get out and exercise more. He earns approximately $45 per hour and has become friends with many of the local dogs in town.

Bentley WIllardson is eight. Although she doesn't have a sophisticated business, she does take neighbors' trash bins in and out and receives $1 for every bin. She has a record-keeping process, and each month she fills out invoices and takes them to the neighbors to get paid.

Little Beckham is only five, and he is not running his own business yet. However, he assists his older siblings and earns money by helping them complete tasks in their businesses.

* * *

A recent study reveals that two-thirds of American families and parents believe their children are spoiled. Whose fault is this? Is it really the kid's fault they're not smart about money?

As Chad writes, "It's understandable why many kids today are a little bit entitled. They have so much more than we had growing up. The idea that we can train our kids to be smart with money, rather than having that entitled mentality, is something I'm deeply passionate about. I want to help empower parents and grandparents, teachers, and mentors. This book is written to help train the next generation to be thoughtfully and financially prepared for their future."

> THIS BOOK IS WRITTEN TO HELP TRAIN THE NEXT GENERATION TO BE THOUGHTFULLY AND FINANCIALLY PREPARED FOR THEIR FUTURE.

Personal Struggles Made Me Stronger

Creating value doesn't always come naturally; I know it didn't for me. I struggled tremendously as a young kid. I was chubby and sported a bowl haircut. I was also the last to learn to talk. I had two fake teeth, and I hated reading. Educators thought I had dyslexia.

All these challenges shaped my competitive drive and identity as "the underdog." Luckily, I excelled at math, which was the main reason they didn't fail me. My teachers didn't want me to fall a grade behind my twin sister, Stacey, who was the smart one. In third grade, a switch flipped. I beat my teacher in chess the first time I ever played it and he taught chess. The other parents realized I wasn't behind, just different.

Then in fourth grade, I started to learn Value Creation. Material value was the first one. I started my first business making beaded gecko keychains and sold them for $1.50. I could make them for ten cents worth of beads and string. Then I hired my classmates to make them for 25 cents. They had a blast making them, and none of them had ever earned any money before. I employed them and made a profit. It was a win-win.

One day, the entire class skipped both lunch and recess because they were making my keychains. The principal found out and suspended me, and my supply line was cut. I went home expecting to be grounded for a week. Instead, my dad took me out to dinner to celebrate. He understood that creating value was the real education, and he wanted me to keep doing it for the rest of my life.

In middle school, I started to realize how to create emotional value for others. I was never the popular kid, far from it actually. But I was perceptive, and I started to dissect what it meant to be a good friend. "How can I help this person?" became my mantra. If a kid was alone at recess, I invited them to play with me. If I encouraged someone, they felt better. If I shared my lunch, they appreciated it. I was the first one to jump in and break up a fight. If one of the bullies started to pick on me, I never let them see me get riled up. I found a way to compliment them or help them with their homework, and they stopped picking on me.

I would secretly go to my teachers and ask if there was anything else they needed help with in the class. It became second nature. I soon became everyone's friend. I had my best friends, of course, but everyone considered me a valuable friend, and they depended on me. Without realizing it, I had become the leader of the class—not the smartest, not the best-looking, not the coolest kid. But the leader. I was the top student, and I received the service award. The school graduation party was at my house.

After attending a private K-8 school, I entered the public high school. I barely knew anyone, so I just ran the same playbook. I was still chubby, and I still had fake teeth. I was the last one in my school to hit puberty. But I knew how to work hard, handle struggle, and create value for others. Before long, I was everyone's friend they could depend on. I became the captain of the tennis and baseball teams, the valedictorian, and a class clown. The good kind.

Struggle builds character. I remember being the slowest person on the baseball team during my sophomore year in high school. I remember it well because the coach gave me the award for "Slowest Person on the Team" in front of 200 parents at the end of the season. I had the highest batting average too, but I guess that wasn't one of the awards.

It was kind of traumatic, now that I think about it, and not a very good coaching move.

I went home, and I felt both humiliated and furious all at once. I decided I was going to be the fastest kid next year. We lived on the beach on Whidbey Island in the northwest corner of Washington State. I decided to run a mile every day down the beach, pulling a hundred-pound log behind me. My dad made me a harness, and that run became my focus. The next season, I became one of the fastest kids on the team. I also hit puberty, which helped a lot. This healthy struggle brought me incredible confidence as I moved into college sports and future success.

The Healthy Struggle Roadmap

When it comes to healthy struggles, sometimes parents don't know where to start. For this reason, we've provided a roadmap parents can use to help their kids start their journey to becoming a Value Creation Kid. Each category is designed to give kids both the capabilities and the confidence to create value in the world.

You can go as deep as you want inside each topic. Bottom line, the goal is to expose your children to various types of healthy struggles. Value Creation Kids have an ever-increasing quiver of capabilities that give them the confidence to succeed. Try to expose your kids to as many of the healthy struggles as you can from the list below. You can start with a simple project or adventure, or dinner conversation starter for each topic and move on from there.

Relationships:

- Family Culture: What does it mean to have your last name, building a family brand.
- Create Your Mission, Vision, and Values for your family, friends, and future
- Reputation: how to build a good reputation and why you cannot afford to lose it
- Friendship: how to be a good friend
- Finding a Good Mentor

- The 4 Rules to Credibility defined by Dan Sullivan, co-founder of Strategic Coach* : show up on time, do what you say, finish what you start, say please and thank you.

Communication:

- Negotiation: How to compromise, create win-wins, techniques, listening
- Persuasion: The art of persuasion, techniques, psychology, tips, why it's important
- Public Speaking: Tips, techniques, and practicing in front of family and friends
- Body Language: What it means, how to have good body language
- Making Conversation: Small talk, being interested, asking good questions
- How to Forgive and Apologize

Mindset:

- Positive Attitude and Constant Improvement
- Abundance Thinking vs. Scarcity Thinking
- Leadership Mentality: How to take more and more ownership of your life
- Goal Setting and Momentum
- Problem-Solving: "We cannot solve our problems with the same thinking we used to create them."—Einstein
- Time Management: Scheduling calendar appointments (dentist/doctor/nails for mom), busyness, chunking your time, etc.
- Teamwork and Collaboration: Adopting a "Who Not How" way of thinking
- Avoiding FOMO (Fear of Missing Out) Traps

- Habits of Success: Be proactive, set goals, prioritize, solve problems, create value, listen, think win-win, and keep sharpening yourself
- Brain Hacks: Tips for memory, speed reading, remembering names, study hacks

Financial Competency:

- Talking About Money at Home: Values, attitudes towards money, openness to discussion
- What is the Economy: Differences between various economic systems, movement of goods/services, supply and demand, chain of production, Gross Domestic Product, and creating value
- Time Value of Money
- Delayed Gratification vs. Instant Gratification and how to practice it at home
- Debits vs. Credits
- Compounding Interest
- Earning
- Saving
- Spending
- Sharing
- Investing
- Protecting
- Borrowing
- Taxes and Insurance

Investing:

- Credit Score
- Financial Planning
- Insurance
- Risk Management

- Blockchain Technology
- Venture Capital
- Trading
- Real Estate

Budgeting and Planning:

- Travel Planning: Plan the next family trip
- Finding your way home from anywhere and how to use a map
- Shopping 101: All the tips for buying food at the store
- Consumerism (Consumer Awareness/Buying Power)
- Setting a Monthly Budget: Reviewing Bank Statements, Balancing a Checkbook

Technology:

- Social Media: Healthy vs. Unhealthy
- Online Security and safety against harm
- Personal Data and how your data is used and sold

Career Prep:

- How to Get a Job: Preparing for a job interview, research, presentation, questions to ask
- Building a Resume
- How to Write a Cover Letter
- Letters of Recommendation
- Internships and Apprenticeships
- Writing Skills - Sales Copy vs. Educational Copy
- Preparing for College: ROI of college, education and career goals, budget and tuition planning, dorm rooms, rent, meal plan, laundry, banking, choosing a college, FAFSA, how to get grants and scholarships

Career Skills:

- Selling Yourself, Selling Ideas, Selling to Others
- Marketing: Content creation, writing, hooks, sales copy, digital marketing, e-commerce
- Engineering: Aerospace, Agricultural, Architectural, Automotive, Biological, Chemical, Civil, Computer, Electrical, Environmental, Geological, Geotechnical, Industrial, Manufacturing, Marine, Mechanical, Mining, Nuclear, Petroleum, Structural, Systems
- Event Planning: Put on an event for 50 people, do a Children's Business Fair
- Nonprofits: How they are funded, how they help the world, mission work, services, research
- Creating a Business LLC
- Financial Planning
- Law and Contracts
- Health and Fitness
- Science and Medicine
- Artificial Intelligence
- Machine Learning
- Software Development
- Digital and Creative Design
- Basic Construction

Practical Skills:

- Physical Fitness and Training
- Nutrition: learning what protein, carbohydrates, and fats do to your body
- Hygiene: Shaving, cleaning your room, showering, brushing teeth, and body odor
- Manners: Tie a tie, etiquette, chivalry, shaking hands, opening doors, making introductions

- Pet Care: Grooming, feeding, cleaning up after, washing, walking, training
- First Aid Basics: How to handle a cold, the flu, cuts, and scrapes, calling 911, what if you see someone unconscious or sibling choking, things to watch out for
- Knot tying: How to tie ten of the most popular knots
- Laundry: Washing, folding, what not to wash, stains, and sewing skills
- Home Improvement: Air filters, turning off water, basic plumbing and electrical, unclogging a toilet, painting a wall, changing a lightbulb, proper closet organization
- Navigating the Kitchen: Basic cooking, using a stove and oven, meal prep, deep cleaning, tiny habits in the kitchen
- Car Maintenance: buying a car, changing a tire, oil, or filters, jumpstarting a car
- Survival Skills and Preparation
- Outdoor skills: Farming, cleaning a fish, hiking, camping, hunting, caring for the environment
- Voting, Democracy, and Government: why they matter and what is civic duty

Our family reviews this list often to see what else we can do to help our kids learn the basics of value creation in the real world. And just like many of the other strategies outlined in this book, the GravyStack app is working to create even more games and real-life challenges that help kids master the topics listed above. Kids and teens will be able to complete these games and missions, earn rewards and badges, and add to their GravyStack skills resume to help them apply for college or a career.

High-Value Takeaways:

- Intentionally removing healthy struggle from your children can significantly increase the time it takes for them to be self-reliant adults.
- Be intentional about designing healthy struggles for your children.
- Teach your kids to create value in the world rather than making it easier on them than it was for you.
- The best education happens when you are intentionally creating more value.
- Learning the value of struggle will make your kids more resilient and less susceptible to negative thoughts and emotions.

PART 3

THE REWARD

CHAPTER 7

HEALTHY COMMUNITIES SOLVE FOR MOST PROBLEMS

Create better conditions to work, live, learn, and play.

Value-creation mindsets and actions create healthier, stronger communities. How do you feel when you are part of a healthy community that supports each other, especially in bad times? How does it feel when you are not part of a healthy community?

Your closest community is your family. Next comes your circle of friends, then your school, clubs, city, state, and country. Imagine if everyone made it a priority to create more value for their communities.

Intentionally talking about the power of healthy communities with your kids is a great first step toward creating a healthier environment. You've already taken a big leap in that direction by establishing your kids' job for the family. When all family members do their job, the family runs better and creates the most value. It's important to talk about why this matters with your children.

149

One reason many kids take their families for granted is that they don't have regular conversations about the value that their closest community brings them. As a result, they often try to please their circles of friends. This doesn't create the healthiest community. Connect these dots for your kids as often as you can. Your goal is to first help them see the value of being part of a healthy community. Then help them understand how to create more value for the community.

> ONE REASON MANY KIDS TAKE THEIR FAMILIES FOR GRANTED IS THAT THEY DON'T HAVE REGULAR CONVERSATIONS ABOUT THE VALUE THAT THEIR CLOSEST COMMUNITY BRINGS THEM.

* * *

The Iroquois Nation, in its prime, consisted of thirteen tribes. They implemented a ritual to help their kids learn from an early age to value the community. When the kids turned five, the tribal members would strip them down to their skivvies, turn them out in the snow, and say, "you are on your own." They wouldn't leave them out in the cold for long, just enough for them to be emotionally imprinted to understand the value of being part of a healthy community. We are in no way suggesting you do this with your children. That was a different time and different culture. However, the importance of community is transcendent. Every family and every culture needs to be intentional about teaching kids the value of healthy communities.

* * *

We all know when things feel right and when they don't. It's hard for people to articulate clearly the most important factors in creating a healthy community. As Lee says, I first discovered the real power of a healthy community and how to intentionally design and influence it while building a business. One of the early companies I founded grew from three employees to over five hundred. This was an aerospace company that repaired and overhauled parts for aircraft operators worldwide. Everything we did was based on creating value, and we incorporated it into all our language. You could ask any team member how they create value for the organization, and you would get a solid answer. Creating value for us was always about creating value for all stakeholders, especially our team members.

As we grew, it was interesting to see the community we created strengthen. Every weekend there were barbeques, and other events employees were inviting other employees to. If someone wanted to participate in an adventure race, it wasn't unusual to have over two hundred team members in blue Able Aerospace t-shirts show up to participate. Everyone got along like one large family.

Over the years, before selling the business, I had dozens of spouses say their husband or wife was a better person to live with after less than a year working for the company. They would ask, "How are you doing this?" We did this by intentionally creating value for each other every day and holding to a clear set of behaviors we held each other accountable to in all interactions. At the top of the list was being honest, respectful, and straightforward.

The real test of a healthy community is when times get tough. There are a hundred-plus examples of employees going through tough times where the other employees stepped up to help in a big way. Examples included employees having unexpected financial challenges, significant medical issues, accidents, and more.

One beautiful soul of a team member named Claudia had a long battle with breast cancer before it took her life. Claudia was not a leader or a partner in the business. She worked in customer support. Out of five hundred employees, over three hundred attended her funeral. The support for Claudia's kids and family continued long after she passed. This happened organically because of the strength of our community.

Another extreme example was a team member named Kevin, who had worked for the company for eleven months when he was in an automobile accident on the way to work one day. Kevin suffered a severe spinal cord injury and was left without the use of his legs. Kevin's job was packaging and shipping boxes. Most companies would have put him on disability insurance and transitioned him into whatever benefits the State had to offer.

We chose to pay Kevin his full wage until he could come back to work. We gave him the option to train in two different jobs he could do from a wheelchair. Kevin chose a job in the supply chain department, adding value by keeping orders flowing smoothly for our customers.

The most amazing thing to me was the dozen employees who spontaneously organized a remodel of Kevin's home. They put in a chair lift so he could get upstairs to sleep in his bedroom, remodeled his bathroom, built ramps, and even modified his car so he could drive using only his hands.

I sold the business eight years ago, and I stay in touch with Kevin and his family to this day. Once you are part of my healthy community, you are always part of it. It's amazing the strength we have from knowing we are always there for each other no matter what.

The lesson for me was that healthy communities really do have each other's back, especially in hard times. The stronger the community, the less outside help it needs. And a value-creation mindset starts it all.

* * *

A true value creator focuses more on solving problems than on setting goals. Solving a problem is concrete, oriented towards others, and much easier to progress towards with accountability from the people it directly benefits.

On the other hand, goals are often win-lose selfish dreams that people set for themselves without any discipline or consistency to actually achieve them.

> A TRUE VALUE CREATOR FOCUSES MORE ON SOLVING PROBLEMS THAN SETTING GOALS.

Most goals can easily become non-value-creating activities that don't provide much to you or anyone else by reaching them. According to the University of Scranton (not affiliated with the critically acclaimed television show, *The Office*), a whopping 91 percent of people who set New Year's resolutions never actually achieve them. Only 9 percent of people reach their goals with discipline, singular focus, consistency, accountability, and a clear roadmap to reach it. But most goals really don't matter enough to people to follow through. That is why using these same tips to solve problems creates much more value to yourself and the community around you.

By focusing on finding problems to solve around you, you naturally begin to create value for the community around you. Here's a goal: "I want to make $100,000 this year" (good luck!). Instead, here's a problem to solve: "I want to break the negative economic cycles in my extended family forever." Instead of losing fifteen pounds by summer, why not solve the problem in your family around how much sugar you consume or the problem of why you aren't moving for forty minutes a day? Maybe organize a weekly running or biking group in the community?

At GravyStack, instead of setting goals for how much money we want to make or how many members have joined our app, we decided to solve the problem of financial illiteracy. We want to eradicate financial ignorance in future generations, and we are asking the world to help us do it. That is something that unlocks massive value for the world around us. It helps us think more clearly about the root of the problem, how to solve the systemic issues, and truly make an impact with our limited time and resources. We do want to see fifty million kids become financially competent by 2030, but that will be a byproduct of our solving the core problem.

Problem solvers also tend to be more self-reliant and dependable inside of communities. They don't drain the surrounding community of material value or emotional energy. Rather, they add to it.

Value creators are trusted, and people turn to them when things get tough. Value creators think logically, critically, and systematically to "work a problem" and find solutions that help everyone involved. How much better would a community be if there were more of these kinds of folks around? The only difference between those people and the rest is their ability to look around and ask, "What can I do now to solve that problem?" And "How can I prevent the next problem from arising as a result of solving this current problem?"

The real leaders of any family or community are the ones who take action to solve problems without being asked. They rarely have the important job title or a fancy desk, and they rarely command or demand others to comply. People follow them because of who they are and how they act. These are our heroes, and these are the best value creators in the world. They embrace hard work and healthy struggles head-on because they know that, in the end, it will produce the most fruit for everyone. Leaders are always moving in the direction of creating better conditions for others to live, work, learn, and play.

A healthy community is one in which all members are focused on creating more and more value materially, emotionally, and spiritually for the rest of the group. Healthy communities solve problems in the community faster and easier with more collaboration. This is because when value is created, it causes an abundance of value, and people tend to cooperate more than they compete. Competition is the result of limited resources and scarcity in a marketplace—too many people selling the same thing, price wars, not enough money or jobs for everyone, or limited time or attention.

We all know what it feels like to be in a constant, unhealthy competition in your family, at your workplace, with teammates, or in your industry. It's not fun, it's toxic, and it's exhausting. This would fall under the unhealthy struggle category.

The only way to create a healthy community is to continuously create value and solve problems in the community. This is a productive struggle because it creates abundance, less competition, and more collaboration to solve even more problems. Each of the following endeavors create healthier communities that solve problems and make the pie bigger.

- a family member who makes some extra cash to lift the financial burden
- the man who mows the elderly woman's lawn next door each week for free
- the kid who finds out that someone is suffering from depression or thinking about suicide, and they find ways to get them help
- the struggling mom who has friends who help with meals or sleepovers during a rough time

Almost every business owner we know started their business to solve a problem in the community, and we love hiring them when we can.

Discuss the communities your children have, beginning with the family and moving outwards. How would you rank the strength of each of these communities in supporting your kids to eventually develop into self-reliant adults? To help you do so, review this list of a few healthy attributes which come from healthy communities.

- They have each other's back in good times and especially bad times.
- They genuinely care for each other.
- They want each other to win.
- They look for ways to add value to other members.
- They help each other in ways that build capability, not enable others by doing for them what they can do for themselves.
- They collaborate and embody team unity.
- They assume each member has the best intent and don't make unhealthy assumptions.
- They do what they say a high percentage of the time.

You may want to add to this list.

Review the communities your kids are part of and rank these healthy community attributes as strong, medium, or weak for each item. For that matter, it may be valuable to list your own communities and do the same exercise. You will likely find that a number of communities listed for your kids are medium to weak when you rank them.

Communities are a continuous work in progress. Just because one community currently ranks as weak, doesn't necessarily mean there is no potential value there. Of course, not all communities are healthy for your kids, and when identified, your kids should remove themselves. Most of the time, however, members of these communities are not intentionally thinking about how to add value and strengthen it. It's amazing what can happen when just one member leans in to intentionally strengthen the community, regardless of its size.

Nothing is as inspiring to a community as one courageous or selfless act performed by an individual for the benefit of the group, especially when it's done by a child. Why do you think that every news station in the country has a spotlight on kids doing great things in the community? It's because when a child takes action to solve a problem, help a neighbor, create a charity, or anything else that creates value for the community, it inspires everyone else to jump in and help!

> NOTHING IS AS INSPIRING TO A COMMUNITY AS ONE COURAGEOUS OR SELFLESS ACT PERFORMED BY AN INDIVIDUAL FOR THE BENEFIT OF THE GROUP, ESPECIALLY WHEN IT'S DONE BY A CHILD.

Kids have an innocence about them that emboldens others, and they have the power to show the adults in the room what to do. Let's encourage our kids to lean into these ideas to strengthen our communities.

The Power of Community

I've been fortunate enough to serve over six million kids and families in my companies since 2011. With Apex Leadership Co., My First Sale, and now GravyStack, I've been blessed to have a front-row seat to see what kids are learning at schools and at homes across America and also what they are not learning. I've studied firsthand how kids learn and what keeps them from learning the right things.

I started Apex Leadership Co. to help my wife raise money for her first-grade students. We would go into schools and teach leadership, character, and fitness; kids raise pledges, and we put on a huge fun run for the community at the end of the program. I've had more pies thrown in my face than any clown who has ever existed.

Over the last decade, that company has grown into the largest school fundraising franchise in America. We have hundreds of incredible franchises in over 40 states, and we've served millions of families and raised hundreds of millions of dollars for schools. It has been the honor of a lifetime to help so many kids grow and thrive.

We've helped kids run over ten million miles. Many of these kids didn't think they could run as many laps or raise as much money for their schools as they actually did. Healthy struggle stretches kids past what they believe is possible. I'll never forget the faces of those kids who ran all thirty-six laps in the time limit. They were ecstatic, running over to their parents to give them huge hugs.

We also created My First Sale to help thousands of kids launch their own online e-commerce site and sell their own products. Once they finished our curriculum on the Five P's of business (Passion, Product, Price, Profit, Pitch), they were ready to launch their business online. The average launch generated over five hundred dollars for each kid. Much of this content has been rolled into some of our mini-games in the GravyStack app.

One of my favorite days of the year is the AZ Children's Business Fair at our local park. We've been putting on these fairs now for thousands of local kids for over ten years. The program has expanded to over 1,400 fairs worldwide now, and it is the perfect way to use healthy struggle to teach business skills to kids using real-life experience. Kids create a product others want or need. They each get their own booth for their business, and they get a chance to sell their product safely to strangers who come to the fair. It's an amazing way to learn sales, profit, marketing, and creating value with your hands.

High-Value Takeaways:

- Healthy communities solve the most problems.
- Be part of and build healthy communities you can count on, especially in tough times.
- The power of critical thinking has a large impact on the health of communities.
- Focus on decisions and actions that improve conditions to work, live, learn, and play.
- Be the positive emotional energy that encourages and develops your communities to create more value and more support for each other over time.
- Win-win can sustain and grow. Win-lose is short lived.

CHAPTER 8

BUILDING A CLEAR PICTURE OF WHAT'S POSSIBLE

Trust the work and continually open up bigger possibilities.

Have you ever wondered what makes the American Dream so attractive and why it has endured over the centuries? One word. Freedom!

Freedom is the most enticing, magical, and explosive idea to ever hit the planet. The benefits are exponential, and it is our greatest superpower as a country. It takes a great deal of struggle to gain freedom, but the rewards are extraordinary.

Creating value is undeniably similar to freedom. It has no end, and it becomes more attractive the more you experience it. Freedom compounds over time. The healthy struggle required to create value pales in comparison to the benefits it offers. In fact, freedom and Value Creation are inextricably linked together. The more value you create, the more freedom you have, and vice versa.

How do we know this?

Over the years, we've mentored and coached countless kids in The GravyStack Method, and we get to see the results first-hand. These kids gain more and more practical capabilities that give them confidence in the real world. Parents report fewer mental health issues at home, less entitlement, less anxiousness, and deeper relationships with their kids.

We've seen dozens of organizations created by kids to help the homeless, save the bees, raise money, and even mentor other students. Countless small businesses have been started by kids to serve their local communities. Their parents are just as ecstatic. One dad sent me a note recently saying that his daughter is now paying her way through college with her small business, and it all began by participating in our business fairs and the value-creation journey.

David Klinkhamer is a prime example of a Value Creation Kid turned into a Value Creation Adult. David's father, Jean, and I started mentoring David ten years ago in this way of thinking. He made $530 at his first business fair, selling mangoes on a stick. He learned how to sell old stuff from around the house online, splitting the profits with dad. He volunteered with Young Life and many other organizations. He made amazing friends who were on the same healthy path, and he learned to avoid the wrong friends. He practiced budgeting, investing, delayed gratification, coding, and how to constantly look for ways to add value. He developed a strong personal faith and a deep care for those around him. He experienced many internships and apprenticeships to find out what he loved and where he excelled.

After he graduated high school, David took a gap year and focused on creating material, emotional, and spiritual value for himself and others. He went on a mission trip, worked for some incredible entrepreneurs, built things, and ultimately got an IT internship that offered him a high-paying job that he loved. As he kept creating value, he kept getting promoted to higher and higher positions. He is now twenty-one years old, making six figures annually as a business intelligence analyst. He started the Magi Initiative to mentor high school students. He just bought his first home, and he recently landed several deals worth tens of millions of dollars to the company. And the best part—he swore off chasing girls in order to become the man that the woman of his dreams would want to marry. Wow! All because he was willing to learn the way of the Value Creation Kid early in his life.

Value Creation Is Contagious

Think about the times you accomplished a challenge. How did you feel? I'm guessing great! If you're like most people, you probably felt as if you could accomplish even more the next time around as long as you put in the work. That's the point of this chapter. Trusting the value-creation work. When you accomplish something truly challenging for you at the time, there's no end to how many times you can repeat the process and build on the value you have already created!

Remember the Value Creation Cycle. The process never needs to end.

THE VALUE
CREATION CYCLE™

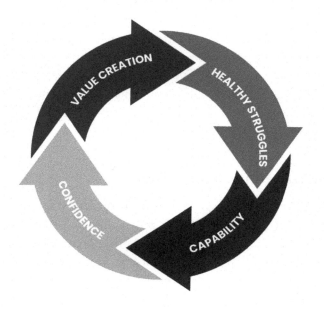

Rather than allowing negative thoughts to swirl in your mind and feeling (and sometimes acting) like a victim when major challenges come up, know deep within your core that it's necessary work for you to create even more value in the world. No one is perfect here, not even the authors of this book. It's easy for us to slip into the "why is this happening to me" mode. If you're intentional about creating value, over time, you will learn to say to yourself, "when I push through this struggle on the other side, I'll create more capability, confidence, and value."

As you learn to trust the work more and more, over time, you'll be able to see further into the future of what's possible for you. We've heard many times that it isn't healthy to live in the space of "I will be happy when." Instead, seeing what's possible in the future based on Value Creation is your compass. Your happiness, fulfillment, and self-esteem are built from the work you're doing now. Learn to love the work and your life right now, even when it is hard.

I Learned to Trust the Work

I remember my journey of creating value and seeing what's possible in the future very well. In the best of times, when I was growing up, my family was at the lowest end of the middle class. My parents struggled financially their entire lives. There was continuous toxic tension in the house, causing one brother to spend a fair amount of time in a juvenile detention center and later, in and out of prison four times before we lost touch. As a young kid, it never occurred to me I would ever even be in the middle class someday.

My parents passed years ago, and as I reflect back, they struggled to raise themselves, let alone five kids. I realized the family dynamic struggles that were so hard on me at the time were never about me. This struggle helped me later in life to have more empathy and communicate more effectively with kids and parents in similar situations. I believe these experiences have allowed me to create significantly more positive emotional value in the world, and I am thankful. Any struggle, healthy or unhealthy, can be leveraged to create more value in the world if we choose.

At around seven years old, a neighbor asked me if I would pull weeds in her garden for twenty-five cents an hour, and I said yes. Back in the late 1960s, twenty-five cents went a long way for a kid! I still remember the cool feeling of earning money from a neighbor (not a family member) who valued my efforts enough to pay me for it. I was so grateful for the opportunity, and I did this work for her many times. Pulling weeds by hand was hard! I wondered if I could do work for other neighbors and make even more money per hour. Where I lived, it snowed a lot in the winter, so I went door-to-door asking to shovel snow off their driveway and sidewalk, which would normally take about 30 minutes, for fifty cents. I just increased the amount of money I was making an hour by a factor of four, and I had many more customers. And yes, I loved it every time it snowed.

From there, I went on to mow lawns and deliver newspapers. By the time I was in junior high school, I was able to buy my own dirt bike, the guitar I'd always wanted, and more. Trading my best efforts for the accumulated best efforts (or money) of others was something I could trust and build on, even with an unstable home environment.

At fifteen-and-a-half years old, I got a job as a dishwasher in a restaurant, which led to being a busboy and then a cook. By the time I moved out of the house at the beginning of my senior year of high school, it was easy to afford my own apartment. I finished high school on my own while working as a cook at night and on weekends. The nights I wasn't working as a cook, my rock band started playing paying gigs. I didn't sleep much, but life was good! I felt as if there was nothing I couldn't do.

I believe the reason my transition into adulthood was easy is because I started the *value-creation struggle journey* early. By starting early—trading my best efforts for the accumulated best efforts of others and building on it each time—I could always see the next bigger step.

I knew I could achieve it as long as I committed to do the value-creating work I had learned to trust. By continually taking the next step in Value Creation, I am now on my seventh company I started from scratch, and collectively I have created hundreds of millions of dollars in value. These companies have made many other millionaires as well. This has been great for my material Value Creation bucket. That said, I believe the positive emotional value I created as a result of building these businesses and working with thousands of leaders is much greater.

You could call this my forty-year overnight success story. I say that because so many who see my success (from their point of view) ask the self-reflective question, "How come this just doesn't happen to me?" Well, it didn't *just happen* to me, either. Rather, it took many years of healthy and some not-so-healthy struggles to continually create more value.

Kids Today Crave Value Creation

People might wonder about the average value-creation mindset of high school seniors today. As part of various youth entrepreneur programs, I've spoken to thousands of high school seniors about the virtues and benefits of starting a business. These interactive conversation sessions were usually with groups of 20-50 kids at a time. At the start of the conversation, I get a sense for where the students are at by asking two questions.

1. If you could meet anyone in the world living today, who would it be and why?
2. What are your chances of being wildly successful in business, and why?

As the kids answered the first question about meeting someone they admire, there was always a bunch of excitement in their voices as they described why. I then ask them what they thought their chances of meeting this person is and 99 percent of the time they responded zero to no chance. Confidence and belief in their ability to achieve great things were pretty low at the start of these conversations.

In response to the question of being wildly successful in business, there was less excitement. About one or two percent of the kids would say they will be very successful, but the majority said it would likely never happen for them for many reasons:

- They don't come from money.
- No one in their family has ever been successful before.
- They won't be able to go to college.
- They live in a poor community.

After the first few minutes of understanding where the kids' heads are, I tell them about my value-creation journey. I describe what my family life was like at a young age and ask whether they thought I had an advantage or disadvantage over them starting out. Some got it right, saying my early struggles gave me a big advantage. Most got it wrong and said I started with a big disadvantage. Learning to put in the work, or healthy struggle, to create value in the world is what we should be teaching our kids.

Then, I describe how I incrementally built on the value I created over time and how it changed my mindset around what is possible, and how it impacted my results. My goal here is to fully connect with the students through experiential stories and conversations, so they better understand how value-creation actions build on themselves.

Since high school, I have been passionate about creating value through business and music (material value and emotional value). On the business side, I went from pulling weeds for $0.25 an hour at a young age to founding companies that collectively have created hundreds of millions of dollars of value.

Value-Creation Mentors Matter

I started playing guitar when I was very young. Actually I can't remember not knowing how to play. I was in the junior high and high school jazz bands, and I played in rock bands before graduating high school. In the 1980s, my band would perform over 300 nights in some years. This was my first business and became my primary source of income back then. Based on these two passions, the two people in the world I most wanted to meet were Jack Welch (the CEO of General Electric who was voted manager of the century) and Steve Vai (who sits above all others in the world of instrumental guitar oriented rock music, in my opinion).

I did some research and found a three-day course Jack Welch was facilitating on leadership and execution, and I signed up. The room was limited to one hundred participants, and most were running billion-dollar plus-sized businesses. My companies, at the time, were so small in comparison; I felt as if I didn't belong. My passion for creating more value through business paid off, though. As the one hundred participants interacted on day one, I could see how they were getting so many things wrong. When I had the opportunity to speak, I presented what I believed to be a better way. Later, Jack intentionally found me at lunch and asked me, "I've done this over thousand times, and no one has ever gotten in right until you. How the heck did you do it?"

I explained to him that if the goal is to create increasing value over time with a business, and you apply math, common sense, logic, and facts, I believe everyone will go down the same value-creation road, encountering the same struggles and insights at each stage of growth. And further, I believed this was the same for someone just starting a business or running a four hundred billion dollar global enterprise like Jack was before he left General Electric in 2001. Jack and I became great friends and business partners over the following twelve years before he passed. I will always miss having conversations with my friend.

If you are passionate about creating value in a particular area, finding mentors to help you take bigger value-creation steps can be invaluable. This is the whole point of the story of my time with Jack Welch. When value-creation passions align, even those persons who have created significantly more value than you will want to help you. Mentoring others to create more value feels great and is something I love doing. For your kids and yourself, who can you identify as a mentor to help each of you create more value in

WHO CAN YOU IDENTIFY
AS A MENTOR TO HELP
EACH OF YOU CREATE MORE
VALUE IN THE WORLD?

the world? I encourage you to embrace engaging with mentors early and often.

Remember, I didn't make the leap from zero to meeting and engaging with one of the top business leaders of all time. It took me thirty years to work up to it. When it happened, it was natural. After thirty years of continually building on Value Creation, it was the right next step. For your kids, at any stage of their value-creation journey, there's always a mentor who can be impactful. Watch them grow under a mentor's guidance and see how their journey unfolds.

Many kids reach out to us for mentorship. These are the ones hooked on Value Creation who are not afraid to ask for help. Your job as a parent will be helping your kids discover the value of all aspects of what is required to create more value over time.

I took a similar path to meet the person I most wanted to meet when it came to music, Steve Vai. Music, for me, is all about conveying emotion. Listening to Steve's playing, I was amazed at the depth of emotion he was able to connect with. Music can be such a powerful force to elevate positive emotional energy to the masses. I believe there's no end to how far you can go to elevate emotional energy through music. I wanted to learn from Steve so I could bring more emotion out in my music. Again, I believe positive emotional energy is the scarcest commodity on the planet, and I want to do my part in elevating it.

I signed up to attend a four-day guitar camp that Steve was leading with many other accomplished guitar players as guest instructors. The experience was incredible, and six years later, I'm still discovering more of my voice on the guitar from what I learned. At the end of each day, Steve and his band would play a set for the one hundred fifty guitar-player campers. At the end of their set on day one, Steve asked for one of us to come up on stage and jam with his band. All around me, I could hear people saying they were not going to go first as I was running up on stage to be first.

I plugged my guitar in, and Steve turned to me and said, "Play something, and we will join in with you." I started playing an original instrumental song I was working on, and they came in at the perfect time, and it sounded like we had played together for years. This was one of the coolest musical experiences I have ever had. When I exited the stage, one of the other campers gave me a video she had taken of my seven-minute jam session with Steve and his band. I was blown away. If you want to see it, go to gravystack.com/book.

The biggest takeaway for me that first week was that there are more than a million ways to play one note, and knowing that has taken me down an amazing rabbit hole. I'm better at connecting the emotions in my head, soul, and heart to my guitar and out to listeners. I used to wonder why I could listen to one hundred guitar players or singers play or sing the exact same song, but only one in each group would make you cry. I never wonder about this anymore. Since that first experience with Steve, I have attended more of his events to help me create even more positive emotional value.

Just like in my business example with Jack Welch, I worked with hundreds of guitar players at various stages of my development before meeting Steve Vai. These are all things you work up to over the appropriate amount of time. We all have someone around us who has taken something we are trying to improve to the next level. And they are almost always willing and excited to help.

In my conversations with teens, after an amazing ninety-minute conversation about the power of building on Value Creation through healthy struggle and the proper use of mentors, I would ask the same two questions again. This time they answered with almost 100 percent certainty that they could meet anyone in the world they wanted to as long as their passions aligned. The answer to the second question was way more powerful. When I asked them what they thought their chances of being wildly successful in business were, they answered that they could start anywhere and go everywhere!

One to five years after speaking with these groups of kids, I would see videos of them talking about businesses they are starting or building. In the videos, they were using the same language I helped them discover in our ninety-minute sessions. For kids, the language of Value Creation and making the value created in the world their primary motivation is powerful, and it sticks.

As I've said before, money and memorization are not education, as so many want us to believe today. Learning to create value in the world is education. Imagine if everything our kids learn today in school, from kindergarten through graduating high school, was taught through the lens of creating value in the world. What would be different? Combine that with changing the language in your home to how each family member creates value for your family and in the world. We would be launching amazing value-creating kids into adulthood who can think critically and continually strengthen the communities they engage with.

When kids begin the value-creation journey and start to see how the work pays off every time in one way or another, most will never get off. As your kids start creating value, help them discover the next steps that will create more value in areas they are passionate about. Even if they don't appear to be passionate about much, exposing your kids to different ways of creating value will help them find their passion.

Your goal is to connect the value your kids are creating today to a fulfilling future for them that they can believe in. It can't be too disconnected. What I mean by that is it's hard to connect the dots from babysitting to running a billion-dollar company. But you can connect the dots from babysitting to someday teaching or having a daycare business.

The key is having your kids envision a future they can believe is possible based on the value they are creating today. If the child is very young, he or she may be looking only six months to a year into the future. As they get older, they can extend that look three, five, or ten years into the future. To be effective, the future has to be believable based on the value your kids have created to date.

This is a journey.

Enjoy it, value it, and embrace the healthy struggles and the emotions that come along for the ride. At any point in time, based on the value-creation progress made, the believable future for your children can change significantly for the better.

The GravyStack Method of learning to create value in the world is designed to make starting this journey with your kids easy. You can't read a book and instantly ooze Value Creation. You can, however, start applying the tools, concepts, and mindset today. You will know you are doing the right work when you can look back in six months and say you've made solid progress.

The GravyStack App will make it easy for you and your kids to get on the value-creation journey and accelerate. It teaches financial competency and the path to financial independence. Both of these are foundational to supporting your family, getting through tough times, supporting causes, and any and all value-creation efforts. The app also can significantly reduce unhealthy financial stress within a family.

Here are three questions to consider as we close:

1. How are you doing in building your forty-year overnight success story?
2. How are you helping your kids discover the beginnings of their forty-year overnight success story?
3. What would be different for you today if you had started this intentional value-creation journey at a very young age?

The good news is you are never too old or too young to start your value-creation journey. The best time to start is now.

High-Value Takeaways:

- Use value-creation successes to adjust your compass to what is possible.
- Build your child's confidence by providing the environment for them to GravyStack their Value Creation.
- You can meet any mentor in the world you want to if your value-creation passions align, but start with people in your immediate circles.
- Create the beginnings of your child's amazing forty-plus-year overnight success story.
- You can start anywhere and go everywhere.

ABOUT THE AUTHORS

SCOTT DONNELL

Scott is a blessed husband and father of four Value Creation Kids. He is the founder of GravyStack.com, the world's first bank account for kids (ages 8-18) that uses games and real-world challenges to teach financial competency to the next generation. The mission of GravyStack is to create fifty million financially competent kids ready to succeed in the real world. Many of the foundational principles of this book can be found in the 100+ games in GravyStack. In 2022, GravyStack won the Most Fundable Company Award in Malibu, CA, out of four thousand business applicants.

Scott is also the founder of Apex Leadership Co., a school fundraising company focused on teaching leadership and fitness to kids across America. Since 2011, Apex has grown into a national franchise with hundreds of franchisees nationwide. Apex has served more than six million students in forty-two states and has raised over one hundred million dollars for schools. He and his companies have been featured in Bloomberg, Fox, NBC, The Wall Street Reporter, and the Entrepreneur Franchise 500.

Scott's other interests include skiing, surfing, technology, biotech, real estate, energy, and water purification. In 2019, Scott founded Hapbee Technologies, a biotech company focused on mental health, which is now public on the TSX Venture Exchange in Canada.

In addition to writing, Scott is a national speaker and family coach for financial competency. He launched the Arizona Children's Business Fair in 2012 and has helped train thousands of young entrepreneurs annually. He also created MyFirstSale.com to teach online e-commerce to kids worldwide. His philanthropic work has focused on the future of education and protecting at-risk children nationwide.

Scott received his undergraduate degrees in Business Management and Theology from Whitworth University and his MBA in Entrepreneurship from the Acton School of Business. He and his family live in Phoenix, Arizona. You can find Scott on social media at @imscottdonnell.

LEE BENSON

Lee, the founder and CEO of Execute to Win (ETW), is one of the world's most influential thinkers on achieving extraordinary results through organizational alignment, decision making and accountability. Over his forty years as a successful entrepreneur, Lee developed his powerful yet practical approach called the most important number and drivers or MIND Methodology™. The MIND Methodology is outlined in his book, *Your Most Important Number*, which is a *Wall Street Journal* and *USA Today* bestseller. Now, Lee and his team at ETW help organizations worldwide work better together to improve what is most important.

Lee started his leadership journey when he became the first employee in a small specialty electroplating services company. After the company lost virtually all its business overnight, he purchased it. With only two employees, Lee immediately set out to build his vision to grow into Able Aerospace, a company with five hundred employees and two thousand customers in sixty countries. Able is known in the aerospace industry as having the best culture, innovation, and ability to execute effectively in a highly complex and regulated environment. In 2016, Textron Aviation, Inc., a Textron, Inc. company acquired Able Aerospace.

Lee has worked with thousands of high school kids on the virtues of entrepreneurship in small groups ranging from 10 to 50 at a time. A big part of these discussions is centered around kids becoming self-reliant adults. Lee also works to improve conditions for K-12 students to learn through A for Arizona, Great Leaders, Strong Schools, and Black Mothers Forum. All these efforts help launch graduating high school seniors into thriving, productive, and self-reliant adults.

Lee is extensively quoted and interviewed as an expert on leadership, execution, and strategy in numerous arenas, including accredited MBA courses, CNBC, and various publications. Lee is also a sought-after keynote speaker, sharing the stage with prominent business leaders like the late Jack Welch and Blake Irving. His innovative, common-sense approach has helped thousands of employees in hundreds of public and private organizations do the right work in the right order at the right time to achieve their most important number.

Lee is an avid guitarist and enjoys vigorous outdoor activities. He sits on several philanthropic boards. Lee also works with college students, introducing basic tenets of entrepreneurship and leadership. He resides in Phoenix, Arizona.

ABOUT THE GRAVYSTACK APP

FINANCIAL LEARNING FOR
THE WHOLE FAMILY

The GravyStack banking app is the practical first step in applying the principles described in the *Value Creation Kid*. GravyStack is the world's first bank account for kids and teens that plays like a game! Kids ages 8-18 play the games and learn to earn, save, spend, share, invest, and protect themselves online.

It's so much more than just a debit card! This epic game harnesses the power of play to teach kids and teens how to have fun becoming financially competent as they learn to earn, save, spend, share, and invest their money. Kids enter the World of Windfall and save its citizens from financial ruin against the greedy tyrant weasel Greedymon and his henchmen before it's too late!

GravyStack provides real-world results almost instantly, enabling families to save money in many of our IRL (in real life) games. In fact, the average GravyStack family saved $547 annually just from one of our IRL games! Another helped families save on average 28% off their grocery bill!

Each family bank account can host up to 5 kids ages 8-18. With GravyStack bank accounts and debit cards, kids and teens gain:

- Access to ATMs nationwide
- FDIC insured bank account

- NO overdraft fees
- NO hidden fees
- NO credit checks

In addition to learning to make and manage real money with the banking portion of the app, each kid competes in the game to build out their resume of skills. When a player completes a financial mission, they earn Grits, which they can use and share in the game.

We also make it simple for parents to set up paid Gigs (jobs) around the house that run on a daily, weekly, or monthly basis. Kids can earn real money by doing Gigs at home or for friends and family! As they earn money, the Money Machine™ makes it fun and easy to see where every dollar comes from and where every dollar goes. You can choose the percentage of every dollar earned to automatically split into your Save, Spend, and Share Jars. Kids learn to invest in real stocks, manage a budget, protect their online security, and even give to charities through the app.

With GravyStack, kids stop asking parents for money because they know how to make their own. You'll have confidence that your child won't overspend, and you'll have peace of mind knowing they are learning lifelong financial independence skills.

For parents, we have created the Parent Elite Community to help families raise Value Creation Kids. This online community offers real-time answers to your questions, weekly dinner conversation starters to help your children learn to create value, and workshops to help you create home gigs, understand taxes, college prep, budgeting, behavior issues and much more. It takes a village to raise a child, and GravyStack is full of like-minded parents who want to see their children succeed.

Start your child or teen on the path to monetary freedom! Visit gravystack.com/go to download the app and begin the process today.

ACKNOWLEDGMENTS

First and foremost, I have to thank my incredible wife, Amy. So much of the credit for this book belongs to you. Your support and love, and encouragement to me to finish this project is what motivated me to complete it. You helped get me through so many of the countless hours of research, meetings, rewrites, late nights and recordings for the book. You took the lion's share of the work at home, taking care of the kids while I was traveling, and bringing me meals in the office. Thank you for being my ride or die, and you are God's greatest gift to me. I love you.

To my kids—Reagan, Sawyer, Owen, and Lincoln. I wrote this book as a love letter to each of you. You are already well on your way to creating incredible value for yourselves and those around you, and my hope is that you find this book to be a valuable tool someday as you raise your kids. We love you very much.

This book would never have been possible without the decades of value creation training from my family. To my mom and dad, Joan and Clark Donnell, for instilling in us the value creation mindset from birth. And to my in-laws, Eric and Tracy Cannon, for raising Amy and her sister to be such incredible humans. And to my extended family, aunt and uncles, Papa Barney and Grandma Joyce, and Papa Doc and Grandma Nancy. You are the definition of legacy, and you have given me the capabilities and confidence to succeed. And to all my awesome cousins, I hope this book helps you with your own families. Thank you all!

To Travis Adams, Justin Dearborn and the incredible, hard-working team of rockstars at GravyStack. You are all building something that will change the world in a powerful way, and I couldn't have done this book without your support. I'm so excited to be on this value creation journey with you all. 50 million financially competent kids—here we come!

To the incredible team at Apex Leadership Co, for helping me learn the power of community and how to make life fun for millions of kids. What you all do everyday is so inspiring, and it is the joy of my life to watch you succeed. I hope this book will only add to your amazing work in schools across America.

To Dan Sullivan and the Strategic Coach community for helping me form these ideas into practical application for kids (especially the Value Creation Kid Matrix), to Joe Polish and the incredible community at Genius Network for helping give me the courage to write this book and get it out to the world, and to Michael Fishman and so many mentors in Consumer Health Summit. Thank you all!

To the incredible community of mentors and friends who have helped me to create the content in this book. To the Children's Business Fair kids, Marketplace One, Camelback Society, Chad and Jenise Johnson, Mark and Ann Timm, Chad and Amber Willardson, Jean Klinkhamer, Chris Smith, Connor Boyack, Tim Tebow, Rich Christiansen, Michael Carlson, Michael Bennett, Caleb Berkery, Carl Casalek, Braden Huyde, Gabe Woodruff, our incredible small group, and the countless other mentors that have helped guide me on this path of Value Creation.

To Drs. Jerry Sittser and Adam Neder at Whitworth University for helping me see who I was made to be and guiding me to entrepreneurship as my ministry. You both changed my life.

To Jeff Sandefer and the folks at Acton Academy, for teaching me the core principles of value creation and how to live a life of meaning. You have made more impact than you will ever know.

To Pastor Rick, for investing so much time in my early years to teach me the value of generosity and kindness. Rest in peace my friend.

To Emily Anne Gullickson and her tireless fight to create better conditions for K-12 students to learn and create value in the world. You are a true inspiration.

To Janelle Wood, Founder and CEO of Black Mothers Forum. Your mission to break the school to prison pipeline is so needed today. You are a rare force for good in the world.

To all of the people and organizations that helped me learn to create value over the years and develop the practical concepts in this book.

To my team at ETW who work tirelessly every day to help organizations of all types create more value.

To Jack Welch and Steve Via for showing me how to create incredible material and emotional value in the world.

To Jim Fletcher, my first boss in my first job at a Coco's restaurant at 15 years old. You believed in me and I have never forgotten what that felt like. Thank you.

And to Kary Oberbrunner, for helping us get this book out to the world. Igniting Souls publishing agency has been phenomenal to help us write and publish this book. Thank you.

NOTES

Foreword

"Youth Risk Behavior Survey Data Summary & Trends Report: 2011–2021." Centers for Disease Control and Prevention. https://www.cdc.gov/healthyyouth/data/yrbs/pdf/YRBS_Data-Summary-Trends_Report2023_508.pdf

Jill Barshay. "Proof Points: A third of public school children were chronically absent after classrooms re-opened, advocacy group says." The Heichinger Report. October 3, 2022. https://hechingerreport.org/proof-points-a-third-of-public-school-children-were-chronically-absent-after-classrooms-re-opened-advocacy-group-says/

Eric Hanushek. "The Economic Cost of the Pandemic: State by State." Hoover Institution. January 3, 2023. https://www.hoover.org/research/economic-cost-pandemic

"Report Details How Gen Z Sees Themselves and Their Future." Walton Family Foundation. June 23, 2022. https://www.waltonfamilyfoundation.org/learning/report-details-how-gen-z-sees-themselves-and-their-future

Generation Alpha graphic courtesy of *Generation Alpha: Understanding Our Children and Helping Them Thrive.* https://mccrindle.com.au/app/uploads/infographics/Generation-Alpha-Infographic-2021.pdf

Note to the Reader

Fearless Soul. "Unforgettable Story of The Butterfly and The Cocoon." *YouTube.* https://youtu.be/dQ26D_Ck158.

Catherine Clifford. "Tony Robbins: This is the secret to happiness in one word." October 6, 2017. https://www.cnbc.com/2017/10/06/tony-robbins-this-is-the-secret-to-happiness-in-one-word.html.

Chapter 1

Gabriel Banschick. "Failure to Launch: What It Is and How to Handle It." *Psychology Today.* March 17, 2020. https://www.psychologytoday.com/us/blog/the-intelligent-divorce/202003/failure-launch-wwhat getshat-it-is-and-how-handle-it.

Alex Hormozi (@AlexHormozi). "You don't become confident by shouting affirmations in the mirror, but by having a stack of undeniable proof that you are who you say you are." *Twitter.* October 29, 2022. https://twitter.com/AlexHormozi/status/1586441477952921600

Gordon Neufeld and Gabor Maté. 2005. *Hold on to Your Kids: Why Parents Need to Matter More Than Peers.* New York: Ballentine.

Nicole DeLaPera (@Theholisticpsyc). *Twitter.* November 16, 2022. https://twitter.com/Theholisticpsyc/status/1592936129002901504

Chapter 3

James Clear. "What Are You Measuring in Your Life?" *Blog.* https://jamesclear.com/measuring.

Chapter 4

Lewis Mandel. "Giving Kids An Allowance Does More Harm Than Good." *Insider.* February 10, 2012. https://www.businessinsider.com/heres-why-giving-your-kid-an-allowance-is-a-bad-idea-2012-2.

Chapter 5

Alisa Wolfson. "Do not save what is left after spending; instead spend what is left after saving." *Goodreads.* Warren Buffett says this is the 'biggest mistake' people make with their money (and psst: it has to do with savings). *MarketWatch.* Aug. 13, 2022 https://www.marketwatch.com/picks/warren-buffett-says-this-is-the-biggest-mistake-people-make-with-their-money-and-psst-it-has-to-do-with-savings-01659574976

Dave Ramsey. "If you will live like no one else, later you can live like no one else." *Goodreads.* https://www.goodreads.com/quotes/19772-if-you-will-live-like-no-one-else-later-you.

Walter Mischel, Ebbe B. Ebbesen, and Antonette Raskoff Zeiss. 1972. "Cognitive and attentional mechanisms in delay of gratification". *Journal of Personality and Social Psychology.* 21 (2): 204–218. doi:10.1037/h0032198. PMID 5010404.

James Clear. "Every action you take is a vote for the type of person you wish to become." *Goodreads.* https://www.goodreads.com/quotes/9624497-every-action-you-take-is-a-vote-for-the-type

Chapter 6

Sam DiSalvo. "5 Huge Lies About Generational Wealth." *Go Banking Rates*. January 28, 2022. https://www.gobankingrates.com/money/wealth/lies-about-generational-wealth/.

Shannen Waller. "4 Ways To Increase Your Credibility And Referability — Fast." *Forbes*. June 12, 2019. https://www.forbes.com/sites/forbescoachescouncil/2019/06/12/four-ways-to-increase-your-credibility-and-referability-fast/?sh=5c0049e34650

https://resources.strategiccoach.com/the-multiplier-mindset-blog/4-ways-to-increase-your-credibility-and-referability-fast

Chapter 7

"91% resolutions fail." 2023. *Enterprise Apps Today*. https://www.enterpriseappstoday.com/stats/new-years-resolution-statistics.html#:~:text=Year's%20Resolution%20Statistics-,Only%209%25%20of%20the%20people%20areNotes%20successful%20in%20keeping%20with,by%20the%20month%20of%20February.

Marcel Schwantes. 2023. "Science Says Only 8 Percent of People Actually Achieve Their Goals. Here Are 7 Things They Do Differently." *Inc*. https://www.inc.com/marcel-schwantes/science-says-only-8-percent-of-people-actually-achieve-their-goals-here-are-7-things-they-do-differently.html

TEACH YOUR KIDS TO BE FINANCIALLY COMPETENT

Scott Donnell
KEYNOTE SPEAKER

gravystack.com/speaking

JOIN OUR PARENT COMMUNITY

Got money questions?
We've got answers.

GRAVYSTACK.COM/COMMUNITY

SMART MONEY PARENTING SHOW

TEACHING YOUR KIDS ABOUT MONEY JUST GOT A WHOLE LOT EASIER.

SMARTMONEYPARENTING.COM

Enjoy Lee's Other Book

BECOME A PARTNER

PTAs & SCHOOLS

AFFILIATE

FINANCIAL PLANNERS

GRAVYSTACK.COM/PARTNER

DOWNLOAD THE GRAVYSTACK APP TODAY!

GRAVYSTACK.COM/GO

THIS BOOK IS PROTECTED INTELLECTUAL PROPERTY

The author of this book values Intellectual Property. The book you just read is protected by Easy IP™, a proprietary process, which integrates blockchain technology giving Intellectual Property "Global Protection." By creating a "Time-Stamped" smart contract that can never be tampered with or changed, we establish "First Use" that tracks back to the author.

Easy IP™ functions much like a Pre-Patent™ since it provides an immutable "First Use" of the Intellectual Property. This is achieved through our proprietary process of leveraging blockchain technology and smart contracts. As a result, proving "First Use" is simple through a global and verifiable smart contract. By protecting intellectual property with blockchain technology and smart contracts, we establish a "First to File" event.

Powered By Easy IP™

LEARN MORE AT EASYIP.TODAY